Elementary Field Experiences

A HANDBOOK
WITH
RESOURCES

Elementary Field Experiences

A HANDBOOK WITH RESOURCES

DONNA I. BENNETT
CHARLOTTE H. MEYER
D. EUGENE MEYER

Delmar Publishers Inc.™

I T P™

NOTICE TO THE READER

Cover design by: Spiral Design Studio

Delmar Staff:
    Associate Editor: Erin J. O'Connor
    Project Editors: Carol Micheli & Andrea Edwards Myers
    Production Coordinator: Sandra Woods
    Art and Design Coordinator: Karen Kunz Kemp

For information, address Delmar Publishers Inc.
3 Columbia Circle, Box 15-015
Albany, New York 12212-5015

Printed in the United States of America
Published simultaneously in Canada
by Nelson Canada,
a division of The Thomson Corporation

    2   3   4   5   6   7   8   9   10   XXX   00   99   98   97   96   95   94

Library of Congress Cataloging-in-Publication Data

Bennett, Donna I.
    Elementary field experiences : a handbook with resources / Donna
I. Bennett, Charlotte H. Meyer, D. Eugene Meyer
        p.   cm.
    Includes bibliographical references (p.   ) and index.
    ISBN 0-8273-5661-7
    1. Student teaching—Handbooks, manuals, etc.   2. Elementary
school teaching—Handbooks, manuals, etc.   3. Classroom management—
Handbooks, manuals, etc.   I. Meyer, Charlotte H.   II. Meyer, D.
Eugene.   III. Title.   IV. Title: Handbook with resources.
LB2153.A3B46   1994   93-38408
372.11'02—dc20   CIP

Contents

Preface

As teachers who have spent many years in elementary classrooms, and have worked most of these years with all levels of students studying to become teachers (first clinicals, second clinicals, and student teachers), we have been highly aware of, and sensitive to, the concerns and anxieties which exist in varying degrees for all of these students. There seems to be so much to learn, so many ways to do it, and such a diversity among today's children.

One desiring to become a teacher must have knowledge in many subject areas, must make skillful use of appropriate methods and materials to deliver quality lessons, and must be ever open to learning. To do this with reasonable success requires one to develop proficiencies in many additional areas. These would include communication, planning, organizational, management, supervisory, human relations, disciplinary, evaluative, instructional, and decision-making skills. Many of these skills will come together simultaneously in helping one execute his or her role. At times the task may seem overwhelming, but it never lacks challenge. The human variable in teaching does not always leave room for pat right or wrong answers on how to teach and how to run a classroom in today's complex and ever-changing society.

This book is directed to the student who has made a tentative career choice and is anticipating his or her first clinical classroom experience. It is meant to be practical in its approach, easy to pick up and read as required or needed, as opposed to a text to study; and hopefully containing a reasonable breadth of ideas.

Since a large number of students has come to the university at the junior year as transfer students, their preparation for this experience is quite varied. We cannot assume what has been experienced by these first clinical students in the areas of lesson planning, case studies, methods, and so on. Therefore, we have compiled a starting framework for this first experience which we embellish with workshops prior to having the students spend time in the elementary classrooms. It is our attempt to put some uniformity and clarity into the students' first classroom experience.

As students continue their experience they will be introduced to additional styles of lesson planning, planning a unit of study, methods of discipline, and more in-depth experiences in the areas introduced during their first clinical experience. The student teaching semester will include current trends in education, mainstreaming, cultural diversity, legal rights and responsibilities, professional ethics, classroom management and discipline, parent conferencing, job application and interviewing techniques, developing a resume, certification information, and some of the social concerns of today and how they impact on both children and teachers. Though many of these areas have been present at all levels of student teacher training they are given more in-depth study during weekly seminars while the student teachers simultaneously experience the classroom teaching environment.

For many, this first clinical is their initial look at the total classroom process. So it seems appropriate to cover a limited amount of material in each discipline upon which they can build as they progress through the program.

An effort has also been made to introduce some of the known subject matter programs currently in use so that students will have some knowledge of these before entering their first school assignment. It is difficult to understand the curriculum format and carry out meaningful observations if one lacks any knowledge of the program and all that is there to observe.

It is hoped that this text will give a basic introduction of the important ingredients of teaching, present some practical suggestions that can be helpful along the way, and be useful in its scope as these students travel through their initial learning experiences and on to their first teaching job.

Acknowledgments

Children are an invigorating challenge, always helping us to keep in touch with the child in ourselves. They are what education is all about, what schools are for, and the reason we are teachers. As we go about planning, our main focus should always be, *what is best for the children.*

In writing this text we have been strongly motivated by our own regard for the value of children in our society and their great need today for well-trained, compassionate, caring teachers. To all the supportive principals and capable colleagues we have worked with over the years; to the growth offered by professional conferences, workshops, and inservice training we were privileged to share in; to the continued learning through salary-supported educational advancement opportunities; to the community and its many educational resources; to the parents who supported us and contributed to our understanding of their children; and most especially to the marvelous and unpredictable bundles of energy known as children who came to us in varying degrees of readiness, we express our sincere appreciation for the enrichment and fulfillment that have been and continue to be ours. All of these people contributed to our growth throughout the years of our working with children and we are forever in their debt.

To Elizabeth Fenwick we express our sincere appreciation for sharing her artistic talent in creating the illustrations.

The authors further wish to acknowledge the loving diligence of a special friend and outstanding secretary, Tanya MaKarrall, who took an interest in this manuscript and gave devoted service through her expert typing and use of computer skills. Her cheerful radiance, as she gave so unselfishly of her own time, was a real inspiration in helping us meet our goal in completing this text.

The authors and staff at Delmar Publishers wish to express their appreciation to the reviewers of this manuscript who made many thoughtful and constructive suggestions.

Sylvia O. Artmann
Dallas Baptist University

Gillian E. Cook
University of Texas-San Antonio

Donna Corlett
University of Portland

Jan L. Hintz
St. Cloud State University

Maxine E. Hirsch
Bucks County Community College

Kenneth W. Kelsey
St. Cloud State University

Karen Liu
Indiana State University

Nell C. Nicholson
Alabama A & M University

M. Kay Stickle
Ball State University

chapter one
Educational Participation in Clinical Experiences

Introduction

The time is here! For years you have been studying and preparing for your future. Now you have made a potential career choice to become a professional educator and have come face-to-face with your first clinical experience in the classroom. It is awesome, exciting, and scary! Yes, it is all of these and more.

Many of you are confident about your choice to become a teacher and are eager to forge ahead, while others may feel a bit dubious and less certain. It is a monumental decision and you need to be somewhat aware of the reasons that influenced you to make this choice. As a student in the elementary grades through high school, you are certainly well acquainted with the environment and the many tasks performed by teachers, thus giving you a sense of familiarity and comfort with this profession. Outstanding role models along the way have had an influence on you, as have parents who may also be working in the field of education. Some of you may feel safer working with children as opposed to an all-adult population which is found in many careers. Some of you are already sure of your choice and sense a high degree of commitment to working with young people toward a greater fulfillment of their developmental needs: physical, emotional, social, and intellectual. Though some of these reasons may not be as solid as others, none is wrong. But it is good to consider them in helping you have a greater sense of yourself and your choice as you approach this first clinical experience.

Throughout this text you will find references made to specific ideas and forms that may not be used in like manner in your situations or even at all. We included them to give structure and clarification in presenting what we feel to be important understandings to you as you encounter your first clinical experience. We further hope that by presenting some references to later clinical and student teaching experiences, and by including resources for your use as both a student and a beginning teacher, we may be giving you a greater sense of the total perspective of which this early clinical is a part.

To give you a bit more assurance and a greater sense of security in this first venture into teaching, you are given an opportunity to fill out a form (see Appendix A) stating your preference of a grade level at which you would most like

1

to work. This form is designed to assist the university supervisor in determining your classroom placement. Every effort will be made to respect your choice, providing the spread of choices of your group is balanced, and there is availability of these classrooms in the building to which you are assigned. At the same time you will be asked to respond to a few questions. Please be specific when answering these as they will be used in a follow-up conference at the end of your clinical experience. At that time we will discover if you have changed some of your beliefs about teaching, had an opportunity to strengthen what was previously a weakness, and found strengths and weaknesses of which you were not aware.

As a student you will be working with classroom teachers, building principals, and parents, as well as students. You should also become acquainted with the many support services available in each school for use by both special-needs students and the teachers. These include the school nurse, social worker and/or counselor, speech teacher, reading specialist, librarian, and learning disabilities teacher. In addition, you should be highly aware of the role that secretaries and custodians play in assisting you as an educator.

It is true that the time you spend in the schools, though brief, will be a major addition to your normal schedule if you do a high quality job. This is *your career choice* and it is the philosophy of these authors to be totally fair and up front with you by helping you experience and discover as full a dimension as possible of your life's work selection. Therefore, we believe that it should be an all-day experience, giving you the full flavor of the total day's program and consequent energies spent.

This experience allows you to see children in a variety of activities and environments, from academic subjects to lunchroom, recess, and special areas; and from their high energy attentive output levels to lower energy and restless times. By being in the building a half hour before and a half hour after the children, you are enabled to have communication time with your cooperating teacher. This assists in planning for the role you will share in the classroom and provides time for clarifying and gaining insights to the events of the day. In many situations, the first clinical experience has been strictly observation by the student. It is the conviction of these authors that you will better your own confidence level by being part of the full day's program rather than seeming like a visitor who appears for only a portion of the day. You also will learn considerably more by being incorporated into the total process of the teaching and learning experiences as is appropriate in the classroom to which you are assigned.

We have found the cooperating teachers to be far more comfortable and receptive to this approach. Also, as a beginner, you may be unsure of what to observe and how to critique what you do observe. Thus, it is far better to get into the process and find out firsthand the many facets of being a teacher. All teachers were once beginners and therefore are usually open and supportive in giving potentially good teachers a place to begin.

Always be comfortable seeking information and clarification. No question is meaningless if it enhances your understanding and learning. This process of thinking about, doing, and then exchanging points of view with your cooperating teacher and supervising instructor provides a learning experience toward becoming a professional educator.

To assist your cooperating teacher in letting you be immediately involved in the classroom process, we provide them with a packet of information before your arrival, including suggestions for appropriate ways to let you participate (see Appendix B). You will quickly learn that teaching is far more than imparting knowledge. Also included in this informational packet to the cooperating teacher will be a letter of introduction from your supervising instructor explaining and clarifying the assignments you are to accomplish in the classroom situation (see Appendix C).

The personal data forms you have previously completed are also included as a means of introducing you and some of your talents and interests to your cooperating teacher (see Appendix D).

As a preservice teacher who desires to become a professional educator, it is up to you to maintain a positive image. Be aware that human relations and an ability to communicate in a professional manner are important to how you are perceived. Attitude, behavior, dress, respect, and responsibility are all vital aspects of such an image. Each of these is addressed herein.

chapter two ══════════
Professional Behavior

Attitude

Creating a positive learning environment in today's highly unpredictable world is a great challenge. The teacher who projects genuine enthusiasm in the teaching process is more likely to successfully engage students in the learning process. By positively reinforcing both students and colleagues, and by demonstrating a willingness to do extra work so that students will benefit, you are clearly exhibiting the type of supportive, positive attitude that is expected and needed from today's teachers.

An important ingredient that blends with attitude is taking initiative. As a well-behaved student, always wanting to do what is right, you have often waited to be told exactly what to do. Be willing to take the first step if you see a need, move to communicate where appropriate, be available to respond to a child's concern, assist in distributing materials, and so forth. If your help is not desired at that juncture, you may be told so, but you will not be faulted for taking appropriate initiative—only for the lack of it.

Behavior

This is a transition time for most of you. You have been a child and a student for many years, striving to fulfill the expectations of the significant adults in your life. On campus you're one of the gang, casual and free. Now you are stepping into an adult role, assuming the attitude, responsibilities, behavior, dress, and conditions of this position. While you are still a student on campus, in the schools you are a young adult and should behave in an appropriate manner toward your peers, your cooperating teacher, and the students with whom you work in the classroom. *Be aware that comments about children are to be treated as confidential information.*

Exchanges with your university supervisor, cooperating teacher, building principal, and parents are to be maintained at a professional level. Remember you are being evaluated as a potential teacher. Use tact and be polite. *Always put forth your best professional qualities.*

Dress

Teaching is a conservative profession. Dress considered appropriate for university courses is usually too casual for clinical experiences in the schools. Plan to dress a notch above what you imagine a teacher should ideally wear, then dress a notch above that. *Remember, should you be dressed inappropriately, the university supervisor, the cooperating teacher or the building principal can terminate your experience.*

Women will find dresses, skirts or dress slacks, blouses or sweaters, hose rather than ankle socks, and flats or loafers (no sneakers) quite appropriate. Men should wear dress shirts, with a tie being optional, and twill or dress pants. Hair should be neat and not distracting or bothersome.

Dressing in a truly adult manner will help reinforce your "teacher feeling."

Respect

As a new person in the classroom you must earn the respect of both the students and your cooperating teacher. *Don't try to be the students' pal.* They will gain greater respect and like you much more for displaying fairness and firmness in a warm manner with all students.

You must indicate that you make decisions and stand by them. You must demonstrate that you can graciously accept constructive criticism. Realize that if you are not given feedback and suggestions for growth, you are not learning a great deal. Be willing to openly discuss both your weaknesses and your strengths with your university supervisor and your cooperating teacher, for only then can they give you supportive help toward becoming a good teacher. Keep in mind that *the good teacher learns something new every day,* no matter how many years he or she may have taught.

Responsibility

As a student beginning the first phase of your teaching career, you are expected to demonstrate responsibility. If you are unable to go to your clinical site, you will be required to make up the time you miss. Many times it is possible to return on another day of the week; this arrangement must be agreeable to your cooperating teacher. It will also be your responsibility to call the school and the university supervisor to inform them of your inability to attend. It is also your responsibility to make arrangements for the return of any teaching materials needed for that day.

During your practicum, you will be entrusted with many materials loaned to you by the cooperating teacher. Please be sure you return all borrowed materials at the conclusion of the practicum. Can you imagine the cooperating teacher's thoughts while completing your final evaluation when he or she remembers you have not returned the materials you borrowed?

By the end of your participation in this all-too-brief but intense classroom experience, giving full consideration to the philosophical guidelines set forth and carrying out the course objectives defined in the next section, you should be highly aware of having made either the right or wrong choice to become a teacher of children.

Following the above guidelines, you will find that you will be respected as a preservice teacher in the challenging field of education.

chapter three
Objectives for Clinical Experience

How well the objectives of the early clinical student teaching experience are achieved will ultimately lie with each student. The clinical requirements provide a minimum set of experiences in which each of you should participate to achieve these objectives.

The clinical experience will provide the student with experiences which will help achieve career objectives. Since this is the first actual classroom experience for most of you, it should also be the time to ask the question: "Is teaching the right career for me?" For most of you the experience will be very positive and reinforcing. There will be a few, however, who will find that the practical everyday concerns of the classroom are often a far cry from the idealistic expectations that led you to embark on a teaching career. While some may drop out of the program at this point, for many it may lead to a rethinking of your career objectives. Many students come into the program with a preconceived idea as to what age level they would like to teach. The clinical experience should give you a basis for modifying your earlier decision. Others may find working with small groups of children much more satisfactory than the total classroom situation; some of you may want to refocus and elect to change your major to special education or another specialty. One example of a successful modification occurred in the case of a very good looking male student who was insistent on being placed in an intermediate classroom. Teaching in the primary grades did not appeal to him as being appropriate for a man. His experience turned out to be very unpleasant, as he was constantly embarrassed by the attention of the fifth-grade girls who had a "crush" on him. The supervisor recommended he visit several primary classrooms taught by men in order to overcome his preconceived notion. In his next clinical experience he requested a primary class and did extremely well.

The clinical experience will provide the students with an opportunity to develop their understanding of the growth of children in all academic, social, physical, and emotional areas. To address this objective you will be required to develop a case study on an individual student. This assignment is intended to sharpen your skills of observation and enlarge your perceptual understanding of the selected child in the areas of social interactions, physical well-being, emotional reactions, and academic performances. You will also be required to prepare a classroom game appropriate for the grade level at which you are working. This assignment not only gives the opportunity to apply knowledge of child development, but implementing it in the classroom will give immediate feedback as to how appropriate it is for that class. One practicum student was very upset on the day she was to play her game with members of a third-grade class. She had played the game with her college roommates the previous evening and they had difficulty with it. In spite of her concerns that it was too hard for the students, she elected to try playing it with them. Much to her amazement they did very well and she had to add more questions to the original game.

The clinical experience will provide the student with an experience which will broaden their understanding of teacher preparation, curriculum, classroom environment, and social and administrative interaction with other school personnel. While the entire practicum will focus on this objective, two of the requirements—to teach a lesson to the entire class and prepare a bulletin board—will certainly broaden your understanding of the amount of preparation required in the teaching of a lesson and of what is needed to maintain an effective and stimulating classroom environment. Again, those of you who become involved in all of the aspects of the classroom—parent conferences, P.T.A., and after-school activities—are going to be much more cognizant of the entire learning experience.

The clinical experience will provide the students with the opportunity to apply the information acquired in the college classroom to an actual classroom situation. The clinical experience now becomes the laboratory for trying out the theories that you have learned in the college classroom. The case study and game preparation give you a chance to apply theories of child development. The lesson plan may evolve from a subject methods class and give you the opportunity to experiment with a new approach. Perhaps more important than any of these is the opportunity to try behavior modifications, positive reinforcement, and other theories of discipline to see if they really have a practical application.

The objectives set forth in this chapter are intended to clarify the requirements of the early clinical experience. Each of these should help you make the transition from the college classroom to the elementary school classroom. This is the time for you to integrate the academic theory you have learned into the practice of your clinical experience.

chapter four
Case Study

This clinical experience requires you to do one case study of a child of your selection from the classroom to which you are assigned. Each child in your class should be seen as a complete and totally separate individual. They could be referred to as cases, in a manner of speaking. You are required to do as thorough a study as is discreetly possible on the case you select.

There are many considerations as you venture into this assignment. The essential purpose of this process is to help you test your ability at getting to know and understand a child with whom you are working. How good are you at perceiving from where a problem child is coming? Teachers need to be constantly aware of each child in their care and be astute at gathering accurate information and using it appropriately in the child's behalf. Hearsay and teacher lounge gossip can be dangerous and often fallacious. Jumping to conclusions based on stereotyped assumptions, such as "He comes from a broken home which is the cause of his problems," can also be erroneous. A top-notch teacher will learn to screen information, learn what is appropriate, and be flexible to change opinions as the situation changes.

You are being asked to do this on one child only; but as a professional, caring teacher you should get to know and understand every child in your care. It is essential to realize that confidentiality is of the utmost importance. Be aware that you must be extremely careful about what is written into the child's records; the open records law makes all written records available to parents. Avoid putting yourself in legal jeopardy as you strive to do a thorough job. You could create a fictitious name for your study and consider it inappropriate to discuss this study with others.

For this assignment, you should keep the names of the student and the cooperating teacher anonymous. In order to have the true experience of developing your own perceptions, it is best to ask your cooperating teacher not to give you background information on students until after you have selected one for your case study. You should not be given this child's background until you have completed your study and summary. When you have completed your study at the end of your clinical experience it would be appropriate to share your findings with your teacher to see if you have gained an insight into that particular child.

You must make a minimum of two observations each day, preferably one in the morning and one later in the day. Make at least one in a special area such as gym, art or music, since many children's behavior changes in different physical settings, interest areas and/or with different instructors. Record and date your observations on the left side of your page, and any reactions or comments you have concerning this behavior on the right side of the page.

Date	Behavior Observed	Comment/Reactions
4/11	Child entered classroom late, interrupting on-going work, coming in with assignment to hand in to teacher, went back out with coat.	Teacher chastised him for interrupting, questioned him in front of class as to his lateness. Child was highly embarrassed. Why couldn't teacher have talked to him later alone?

It is all right for you to raise questions about the teacher's actions in various situations. As you are in the classroom longer, you may better understand the reasons behind the teacher's responses, or you may realize that you would prefer to handle a situation differently. That's part of learning.

There are several good reasons to be aware of and comfortable with the case-study process. The first objective is to become more aware of the unique histories, circumstances, and needs of each student. The second objective is to become adept at using the information you have to respond individually and appropriately to the needs of each child.

Gathering this information is a multi-faceted process and requires extremely good judgment. Making inferences based on factual input from reliable sources must be done discreetly and then be properly applied. For example, a child from a broken home does not automatically have problems. He or she may be far better off than the child who lies awake each night hearing his or her parents argue. Nor is the child of working parents necessarily lacking in quality attention. On the other hand, *some* children from broken homes and *some* children of working parents may be adversely affected by these situations. Be conservative when making generalizations.

Driving around the community to learn where your students live (when you are a full-fledged teacher) can give you a little more insight to their backgrounds. A student bused to school from the country may have limited social contacts with peers. Children from apartment complexes may experience a different style of living than children from single-family homes in the suburbs. But, again, cultural and/or economic differences do not necessarily demonstrate the quality of love and concern that a child receives at home.

Another way to gain greater understanding of your students is through parent conferences, especially of those children who give you more immediate cause for concern. It does not have to be grading time to have a conference. It is good to deal quickly with the concerns that disrupt constructive learning to better meet the needs and capabilities of all your students.

During your clinical experience you may have occasion to learn some of the methods used by your cooperating teacher to gain greater understanding of each student. Parent conferencing is in wide use today for reporting academic progress of students. When used well, it is a very effective way to gain insight into the behavior of individual students, and in developing a stronger cooperative working relationship between home and school. It will not be possible to share in this conferencing process as a beginning clinical student, but you can learn about it and will probably encounter it firsthand as you progress through your next clinical and/or student teaching experiences.

Another way to gain a fuller understanding of each child is to have a private interview. This can be accomplished by inviting a child to visit you during recess or in a special class such as music, art, or gym. Most children see this as a privilege, and benefit from the individual attention. The environment for this process should be well structured by you while creating a warm, comfortable, and conversational environment for the child.

What type of questions do you want to ask the child? You may already know the answers to some questions, but they serve as good openers to other information that might help you. Following is a list of possible questions you may wish to ask. They should be rephrased by you to create a conversational tone rather than a quizzing format. For example: "Let's see, you must be about seven years old." Instead of "How old are you?" Some of these questions might be more appropriate for older children. You will get a much better feeling about the children's responses if you question them individually and orally rather than getting responses in writing. Always honor their right *not* to respond to any particular question.

1. What is good about being the age you are?
2. Name at least one important hobby or interest of yours. How much time do you give this activity each week?
3. What is your ethnic heritage (race and nationality of your parents and grandparents)? How important to your family is this heritage?
4. Where do you live? Is it a house, apartment, mobile home? How long have you lived there?
5. With whom do you live? Do you have your own room? If not, who shares it with you? Where is your favorite spot at home?
6. What do your parents do for a living?
7. How do you usually spend your after-school hours?
8. With whom do you eat lunch?
9. Who are your three best friends? Tell a little bit about each.
10. What responsibilities do you have at home? How do you feel about them?
11. Name one thing you do very well.
12. What are your favorite foods? TV shows? Colors? Academic subjects?
13. What is your astrological sign? Does it mean anything to you?

14. How much spending money do you have each week? Where do you get it? How do you spend it?
15. What is your major ambition for the next year?
16. What occupational plans have you made for your future?
17. What embarrasses you?
18. Who, if anyone, helps you with homework?
19. What adult are you closest to? Describe this person briefly.
20. Do you consider yourself a leader or a follower? Why?
21. What books have you read in the last month? Which had something important to say to you?
22. What magazines or newspapers do you read regularly?
23. How did you spend the last two Saturday afternoons?
24. If you could go anywhere in the world tomorrow, where would you go?

After completing your final day's observations you need to summarize your study. Imagine yourself as the teacher and explore some questions you may have. If this child were your responsibility, what would you do for him or her? What information could you gain from a parent conference that would help you do your best for this youngster? What kinds of testing might be indicated and what special services are available to give you added assistance in meeting this child's needs?

Case Study Examples

To help you understand case studies and how to set them up, we have included examples that were done by early clinical students. They are not faultless and should not limit what you can do. You are required to make two observations daily; these have made only one, which is too limiting. It is apparent that none used an interview process to gain more extensive information about his or her case study. Summaries should be more adequate.

Accompanying the examples are instructor comments and questions to help you learn how to delve into your case study. You cannot be expected to answer all of these questions, but you should raise questions that as a teacher you would explore further. Do the best you can and list all the possibilities that occur to you in your own study. Certainly no one should draw any hard-and-fast conclusions, but always be exploring and fluid.

Case Study One—Third-Grade Girl

Because Mrs. Bower's class splits up for reading and math, I chose a student who stays in her room for both subjects. She is one of only two students who have Mrs. Bower's for both subjects.

Date	Behavior	Comments
4/3	Rosita was the first child to approach me for help.	This child seems outgoing and not shy. She unhesitantly approached me for help the first day, whereas most of the other children were not quite sure about me yet.
4/5	She was content being alone on the playground. She does not socialize much with others. She approached me a couple times on the on the playground but, in general, she seemed very content with her own company.	I was able to go outside for recess. This child plays alone for the most part, but she does not seem to mind it.
4/10	In math class, she is one of the brighter students.	I watched her during math, in which she is in the higher level group. During time tests (30 sec.), she was the first one done (app. 15). She also whizzes through all of her math exercises and keeps herself busy after that. Her accuracy in math is always near 100 percent.
4/12	Very good reading abilities for her group—scolded for excessive talking.	Although she is in the slower third-grade reading class, she also excels. She seems to be one of the better readers in the class. As in math, she is always very eager to answer questions or do work on the board. Today was the first day she was scolded since I have been there. She and her neighbor were very talkative today and she was scolded by the teacher a couple times.
4/17	Difficulty in reading comprehension.	Today I did my lesson. This child was very interested and attentive, sharing stories of her own that related to the story. Although, when I asked

4/17 *cont'd*		comprehension questions, her answers were not quite on the right track. I have also noticed in some of her homework that she is not strong in reading comprehension.
4/19	Approaches me for help but answers her own questions.	The student approached me on two different occasions during work time for reading. Each time she approached me, she read the question, answered it herself and looked to me for reassurance. I noticed in both math and reading she is quite eager and accurate in responding. I think she just feels the need to be reassured that she is correct.
4/22	No noticeable behavior.	Today this student was generally well-behaved and average. She was quiet and did well with all of her morning work. She had fallen on the playground last week and hurt her head. She had quite a large scab today, so I assume that it probably hurt pretty badly when it happened. Also today, Mrs. Bower shared with me that this student was the youngest from a very large family and seemed to be more immature than most third-graders. She also said that she pouted a lot when she did not get her way. I told Mrs. Bower that I did not see her exhibiting these behaviors. Mrs. Bower said that as the year has gone by she has gotten better about it.

Instructor's Response

You have made no summary of your case study presenting any of your perceptions as a result of your observations of this child. You indicate that this girl does not socialize and is content to be alone on the playground. Do you feel that as a teacher you should have a concern for her social development or lack of it? Is she getting any encouragement from the teacher in making friends? Do you know for sure that she is truly *content* to play alone or just doesn't know how to do otherwise? I would want a parent conference to learn more about her social contacts in her own neighborhood. Does she ever have friends over to play? Is she over-sheltered, which might account for some immaturity in developing socializing skills? We need to consider all dimensions of a child's development (physical, social, and emotional) if we are to achieve the highest potential in academic areas.

Case Study Two—First-Grade Boy

Date	Behavior	Comments
4/3	Can't sit still; constantly talking.	Michael doesn't listen to directions. Once he gets on task, he completes it.
4/5	Michael instigates confrontations with other students.	He doesn't deal well with group activities on the floor. Needs his own space.
4/12	Talking while teacher is giving instructions.	Teacher had to separate him from the class twice for disruptive behavior.
4/19	Michael did well when group was interacting on floor.	Michael was very excited about the rabbit that came to visit. He was very cooperative in the group.
4/26	Paid attention to the teacher's directions and stayed on task most of the time.	Michael is being much more cooperative in class.

Summary

Michael has been observed by the school principal, psychologist, and social worker. According to his teacher, he had four to five outbursts a day. When I first observed him, he was very restless, constantly talking, and in motion. In the four weeks I was there I only saw two outbursts. Michael has come a long way in learning to control his temper and interact with his peers. This week there will be a meeting with Michael's parents and all the people who have observed him to decide if he should be placed in a behavior-disorder classroom. I do not think Michael should be removed from the regular classroom. His progress shows he is capable of adapting to the classroom situation.

Instructor's Response

Remember, you have observed this boy for a very short time and for only two days a week. Perhaps the Pupil Personnel Service Team will not recommend him for a special class, but if they do, it will not be done capriciously. If he has shown improvement, perhaps this is a vital time to give him more personalized assistance in a small group where he can benefit from the added support and return more quickly to the regular classroom. I can only conjecture, but I am trying to let you see that there are always several ways to look at the same picture.

Case Study Three—Third-Grade Boy

Date	Behavior	Comments
2/20	Patrick is out of his seat again. His body is in the desk frame but he is constantly sitting on his feet or kneeling on his knees. Mrs. Smith is reading a story during "read and rest" time. He is not interested in the story, but is interested in the activity of the other children. The others do not pay much attention to him.	Patrick is a child with a lot of energy. He is not a behavior problem from what I can tell. Sitting in a seat does seem to be a problem, though. He is a very sociable child, which is a disadvantage to the children around him.
2/22	Today Patrick was observed outside his regular classroom. The third-grade classes met in the music room to listen to a guest speaker. Patrick, initially	Patrick is a very excitable student. He enjoys being able to move about. A small move such as the one made causes him to make quite a commotion. Patrick's attention span is quite

2/22 *cont'd*	raced in to the room, finding his way to the front row. He was quite excited, as were the other children. While the dentist spoke, Patrick listened for most of the time, but talked to his neighbors frequently. When he received the pictures that were being sent around he studied them carefully at first, but then started talking to the student next to him about them. He laughed at the picture and was reluctant to pass it on.

short if it requires listening. He has better behavior when he can touch, see, feel, and do. Many of the children cannot sit and listen for very long, but Patrick needs to discipline himself better to keep pace with the rest of the class.

2/27	Patrick is talking to his neighbor when he should be working on his language work. He is keeping his eye on me, but this does not stop him from talking. Even when I point-blank look at him, he continues to talk. Only after I went and stood by him did he stop talking. He is now staring off into space, not even interested in his work. Finally, he focuses his attention on his work.

It takes a long time for Patrick to settle down. He tests authority a bit more than the rest of the class. Patrick needs a little more motivation to get him started. He is on task once he gets started.

3/1	Mrs. Smith is doing a reading lesson. Patrick is very fidgety. His shirt sleeves are consuming most of his attention. He needs to blow his nose. When I ask him if he needs to get a tissue he says he does not. His feet are in constant motion,

I am beginning to think that Patrick might be bored with his school work. This might explain his restless behavior. I am surprised that when I suggested that Patrick get up to get a tissue, he didn't jump at the chance to get up.

3/1 *cont'd*	either tapping the floor or swaying. He yawns quite loudly. When called upon, he is quick to respond.	

3/8	Today I observed Patrick in the school learning center. Two third-graders combined to watch a French show for a half hour. Patrick talked through most of the show. He was reprimanded and then moved. Patrick is sitting on the floor coloring now. He is reciting the French words with the program. Spread out on the floor, he is quiet and participating.	Patrick does not like boundaries. When confined to an area he becomes restless and talkative. He is fine as long as he is not cooped up in his desk.

Summary

Patrick is not a behavior problem, but rather he is a typical eight-year-old boy. He is a social and talkative child. This does not interfere with his school work, but it does interfere with the others' sometimes. School work does get done by him although Patrick does have a hard time getting started. This particular class is very organized, and perhaps he might be less restless in a class that is less structured. Through conversations with Patrick I have determined he is a very interesting child. He always has much to talk about and truly enjoys sharing with others. I do not think he intends to be disruptive.

Instructor's Response

You have a refreshing understanding of this boy. We need more educators who can accept higher energy behavior as normal. This can be very normal and desirable. The next step is how to channel some of this sociability and energy into a positive contribution in the classroom setting, both for the benefit of the child's learning opportunities and the class as a whole. Your suggestion of a less structured environment would be one possible solution, although one would need to monitor his lack of organization when getting started on a task. Too often a child of this type is stepped on for disrupting and annoying others, and can have his confidence undermined and his enthusiasm turned to negative energy output. That can be disruptive while hurting the child. It is far better to spend some additional effort early to find positive ways to employ the child's interests, energies, and abilities. You have a good insight into the make-up of this boy.

Case Study Four—Second-Grade Boy

Date	Behavior	Comments
3/16	Michael and I worked on different spellings of of the long "o" vowel, such as boat and note.	Michael began second grade not knowing any letters of the alphabet. He is very far behind and spends part of every day in the resource room. Today we worked together after his time in the resource center while the rest of the class did their standard achievement tests. He understood the concept of using oa, a_e but didn't know how to differentiate between the two.
3/18	Michael asked me if I would test him on his spelling words that we worked on Monday.	He really surprised me when he initiated the quiz. Originally he was supposed to be tested on Friday (3/20). He told me he studied the night before. I could tell he was really trying, but he does not stay on task for very long. He got eight out of ten words on his quiz.
3/23	Michael was absent today.	
3/25	Today during music Michael was very disruptive. He was constantly bothering other students near him. When I moved and sat next to him he continued his bothersome behavior. Later we played my game together and we had more time to talk.	Michael and I talked for a long time today. I found out that he was absent Monday because he hurt his toes. He said he got mad at his friend and kicked a radio; now all of his toes are black and blue. He also told me that his new home is much more peaceful

3/25 cont'd		than his home where his grandfather still lives. His attention span seemed much shorter today than in the past; it was very hard for him to stay on task, but I still feel he is trying very hard.
3/27	Today Michael and I played Tangoes, a game where you fit seven shapes together to make different figures.	I found it very interesting that Michael confused some shapes and inverted them. If a triangle was on the left with a point at the top he would either put it on the right or have the point facing down. He didn't do it all of the time, but it was very interesting to notice.

Summary

Through observing Michael and from what Mrs. Jones has told me, I can tell Michael has a lot of problems. I think that many of them stem from home. Because he leaves during part of the day, I assume he has been observed by professionals. However, I do think Michael has made a lot of progress in a short period of time. I doubt if he will ever be able to catch up with his peers.

Instructor's Response

Don't assume anything. What are Michael's problems? All I see from this is that he is way behind, doesn't know basic facts (letters, etc.), and has trouble paying consistent attention.

Hold a parent conference during which you learn all you can about Michael. Such information as ages of sitting, walking, and talking could be helpful. You need to learn whether he has always been slow in development. Has he had preschool experience, is family highly mobile, what is their apparent interest in their child's education? Then enlist their help as appropriate.

Has Michael been tested for psychological learning disabilities and ability, motor dexterity, etc., then staffed and totally reviewed? If he has not, he certainly should be; if he has, what are the results? Is the present set-up working—if not what can be tried for improvement?

What is the cause of his disruptive behavior? Is it connected to an unsettled home life, some type of abuse, some type of injury—drugs (parental)? Or is it more related to his lack of social acceptance? Many children this far behind do not fit in and do not know how to get in. It is vitally important for him to have a feeling of belonging among his peers. Many times children's restless non-attention is related to thinking about who will play with them at recess—then they go into some disruptive, unacceptable behavior in search of the attention they need so badly, not really able to discriminate the positive from the negative. Michael has many things in need of support—emotional, social, and probably physical; and with support Michael could give more attention to the learning of academics if there is no serious learning disability.

Case Study Five—First Grade Girl

Date	Behavior	Comments
3/16	Sarah hit her leg on the playground this morning. She demands special attention during her gym class by bringing her ice pack and refusing to participate even though she was fine.	Sarah seems to enjoy attention Whenever she is given the chance to receive it, she demands it!
3/18	Today, Sarah is paying very close attention to the math lesson. She volunteers her answer about halves. She is the first child to finish her math workbook sheet.	Sarah enjoys math. She feels very successful with it and enjoys being praised. She has come a long way with math so far and is reinforced for her progress.
3/23	Sarah is having trouble keeping quiet this morning She is constantly interrupting the class and cannot sit still.	Sarah is very restless because she was late for school today and is anxious to share her story with anyone around her.
3/25	Sarah enjoys singing during music, but cannot sit still during the instructions.	Sarah has a hard time staying on task. She is very energetic and always has to be doing something.
3/30	Sarah reads the poem of the day without being asked to. She is successful.	She enjoys reading and is excited when she can be successful at reading.

Summary

Sarah has been working on a behavior management program with her teacher. Each morning she writes down a good goal for herself. Every time she is disciplined, she gets a check mark on her goal paper. At the end of the day these marks are added up. If she reaches her goal, she is rewarded. This method seems to work well with Sarah's behavior problems. Sarah is having fewer problems everyday using this plan. Sarah's behavior has improved greatly since I first observed her, but still needs work. Sarah is a very bright student, but gets distracted easily. She comes from a large family and always has much going on. For this reason, she has trouble staying on task, but she is improving her attention skills.

Instructor's Response

What is her basic problem? It seems that much of her behavior is a plea for needed attention. She needs to learn that you really enjoy giving her attention, but will ignore her when she is demanding attention through unacceptable means. For example, I would have given her the choice to stay by herself in the classroom with her ice pack or go to gym to participate with no ice pack. That makes her think. She probably does not want to be alone without any attention, so she is forced to give up her faking for attention. Then follow it up with praise for being such a good sport.

Case Study Six—Kindergarten Boy

Date	Behavior	Comments
9/21	Ken interacted well with the other children. He was sitting attentively during story time. During class discussion, he was sitting on his knees and waving his hands impatiently to get the teacher's attention. Ken finished his work before the instructions were given. He did not put his school supply box away when he left the table.	Ken was well-behaved during the activities. He seemed to interact well with the others. He seemed to be in a hurry most of the time. He quickly finished his work and left the table early. He would sit attentively, but would get impatient if he had to sit too long.
9/23	During story time Ken looked around the room and not	Ken seems to have a short attention span. He seems

9/23 cont'd	at the book. Ken was running to the line and had to go back and sit down.	to be easily distracted if things do not interest him. He works well with others during playtime. He is not very talkative. If the teacher does not notice his hand up, Ken waves it and sits on his knees until she notices.
9/28	Ken would sit on his knees and wave his arms to get attention.	I noticed that Ken interacts well with his peers during playtime. I had a chance to talk to him during the art activity. He always rushes to finish the activity. I asked why, and he told me that he thought of the work as a race. He would rush to be the first one finished, even if his work was sloppy.
9/30	Ken was sitting attentively during story time and independent seat work. Ken and other students were pushing each other while standing in line. He immediately stopped when I looked at him, but would continue when I looked away. They stopped when the line started moving.	Ken works well with others. He can play games with others and cooperate. I watched him playing dominoes with another student and he was patient and waited for his turn. I feel that his behavior in line was due to impatience and the fact that the line was not moving. Both students involved were encouraging each other and thought that the pushing was a game.
10/5	No observable behaviors. Sat attentively during lesson. Ken cooperated well when asked to pass out papers. Ken stared off into space during the story.	Ken seemed more relaxed and attentive today during the lesson. He did not seem to be interested in the story. He was frustrated when I asked him to go over the math problems that he had done wrong. Even though he knew the correct answer, he would guess.

Summary

From what I observed, Ken is like any typical five-year-old boy. He interacts well with others during classroom activities. He seems to get easily bored with an activity, if it does not interest him. He is always in a hurry to finish the activities. When I talked to Ken he told me he pretended everything was a race and he wanted to be the first one done. Sometimes his work is sloppy, not because he does not know how to do it, but because he is always in a hurry. He is a bright child and has an understanding of the material. I think if he slows down a little the quality of his work will improve.

Instructor's Response

You have done some good observing. I would like to add that these children are kindergartners in their first month of school. They are not used to sharing attention with so many others. The limitations of seat work, circle sitting, etc., can wear pretty thin on healthy, active children.

You were in a lovely, big room with lots of equipment and a fairly relaxed teacher. How did you feel about the highly organized, regimented environment? What about allowing for expression, movement, creativity, dress-up, pretend play, water tables, paint easels, big trucks and blocks, a sand table, play house area, and rhythmic activities? In other words, where are any of the experiential activities that might make a little mess or create a bit of noise? Kindergartners are still children with wonderful curiosity and need social interaction along with active playtime. Readiness work is an important part of the program, but it needs to be balanced with the other developmental aspects of these young children.

You have done a thoughtful study and have shown some good perceptions. My comments are intended to give you additional dimensions to think about.

Case Study Seven—Sixth-Grade Boy

Date	Behavior	Comments
9/21	Keith raises his hand an excessive number of times. Many times he has no idea what the answer is. Also, he appears to be extremely unorganized because he cannot find his worksheets when they are to be handed in.	Keith appears to need constant attention, even if it embarasses him, such as guessing at an answer when he has no idea. Also, his problem with organization can be linked to his desire for attention.

9/23	Keith continues to search for attention. I have noticed that in his attempts to find attention he sometimes disturbs those working around him. Reprimanding him for his behavior works; however, he seems to pout and not pay attention afterward.	When the teacher disciplines Keith he does behave better, but it also makes him stop paying attention. This leads me to believe that discipline somewhere between could be effective.
9/28	Today I had an opportunity to talk to Keith. I discovered he was an only child, and discussed some of his interests. Because I gave my lesson plan on the presidential election, he was anxious to show me how knowledgeable he was about the candidates.	Keith is an extremely knowledgeable, outgoing student. However, I do feel this needs to be channeled more into his schoolwork. I also noticed that Keith is beginning to show an interest in girls, and this could be a major factor as to why he is trying so hard to draw attention to himself. It could also be a factor as why his schoolwork is not always up to par.
9/30	Today Keith forgot to do a homework assignment. When the teacher confronted him about it, he attempted to lie his way out of it. After she disciplined him he became discouraged and no longer participated in the lesson.	The negative reaction Keith had to not doing his homework leads me to believe he is extremely concerned with his schoolwork. It also makes me believe he will straighten up when he does not need as much attention.
10/5	Today Keith seems to be behaving better. His hand remains up on most questions, many times without knowing the answer. He also appears to be more on task, and concentrating better.	Keith's better behavior could be linked to a change in seating. Instead of being seated in the front of the room, around more sociable boys and girls, he is seated by less sociable kids in the back of the room, where he does not have an audience.

Summary

After observing Keith for five days I have concluded that he has a few problems. However, they are not serious and will begin to diminish over time. While Keith is a bit overanxious when it comes to answering questions, and may not always be on task when it comes to homework, he is an extremely knowledgeable student with a large amount of energy for learning. If Keith's problems can be attributed to one aspect, it would be that he is an only child and is used to being the center of attention at home. The easiest way for this to occur in the classroom is for him to constantly ask or answer questions regardless of whether they are right or wrong. The easiest solution would be to find a happy medium between giving Keith enough attention, and reducing the number of times he disrupts class.

Instructor's Response

Usually children who have attention needs met within the home do not need as much in other settings. However, if parents are busy and preoccupied, he could feel a greater need for more attention that says, "You are important to me." He certainly is exhibiting symptoms of attention need. Now that you have identified this need, a more conscious effort should be directed toward reinforcement when it can be for positive behaviors. Discipline is also attention, but is a negative response, and should be used as little as possible. What constructive goal is served by disciplining when (as you have observed) it puts him off track from giving attention to the task at hand? It further serves to give him a sense of rejection. He needs the sociability of friends and peers as an additional reinforcement. Reading between the lines of your comments I question his sense of security in his peer relationships. Just another reason for his bids for attention. And when one is hurting, negative attention is better than no attention.

It is a constant challenge to be a sensitive, caring teacher trying to understand and then meet the needs of each child. It seems that in an effort to maintain quiet and order, Keith is moved away from what he really needs—sociable kids. How about creating some cooperative learning situations in which assignments can be done in groups, which also allow for modest sociability? Then, at other times, he can have a quiet environment in which to work alone. You demonstrate some good understanding of this young man's needs.

Case Study Eight—Third-Grade Boy

Date	Behavior	Comments
9/21 cont'd	Nathan leaves his chair and walks to the pencil	The substitute teacher uses the verbal instruction,

9/21 cont'd	sharpener without a pencil in his hand. He does not talk to any of the other students while out of his seat. Nathan is supposed to be at his seat working on his mini-math problems (the rest of the class is doing the problems).	"Nathan, please go back to your seat and finish your work." Nathan appears to have heard the order, but does not go back to his seat. The teacher restates the instruction. This time Nathan complies. I chose to go to his desk to see if he needed anything. When he told me that he did not understand how to do the problems, I showed him. He finished his problems and did not leave his seat the rest of the math time.
	Nathan is observed in the computer room. He listens to the computer teacher and follows the instructions completely.	Nathan is interested in the computer and demon-strates this by engaging in the planned activity.

9/28	Nathan engages in a form of physical aggression by hitting his desk with a rolled piece of notebook paper. The class is part-icipating with the teacher while she does math on the overhead. The teacher asks the class to find the answer to her question by looking at the number chart on the screen. Nathan does not look up at the screen, but continues hitting his desk with his paper.	It has become quite obvious that Nathan does not enjoy participating in math dis-cussion. I have noticed, though, that he seldom asks questions when he works in-dependently on his problems. It is hard to tell if he has difficulty with the assignment or with the instructions.
	Nathan is working inde-pendently on the type-writer. He is allowed to type while the rest of the class works on science and health. Nathan asks me	He shows initiative in working on his project. He also does it in a manner that does not disturb the class. Nathan does not appear to mind asking for

9/28 *cont'd*	to come over five different times to correct his spelling. When he does not know how to start the spelling, he whispers for me to help him.	help. He is confident with his typing and proudly shows me his work.
9/30	Nathan is instructed to sit down after he rises to sharpen his pencil during a math lesson. He hesitates a few moments and then sits down. Nathan is then told to turn his seat around so he can see the chalkboard. He moves his chair but not enough so he can see the board completely. Nathan asks questions during the health lesson and gives answers to the teacher's questions. He completes his food guide pyramid and silently reads the rest of the time.	This behavior is a repeat performance. Nathan takes it upon himself to do what he feels is necessary. After this, Nathan raised his hand and answered the math question correctly. He received verbal praise from the teacher. Nathan has to be ready for the lesson to become actively involved. Nathan enjoyed the lesson and understood the instructions. He was one of the few to get started and finished right away. To me, this showed that he can become involved more in class time and classwork.
10/5	Nathan needed help today with his reading skit. He had difficulty with several words. He asked me what they were. When I started to sound them out, he finished them without my help. I praised him and he smiled his thanks.	Nathan needs help getting started. When he learns a new word, he remembers it the next time he reads his part in the story. I believe that once Nathan is sure of himself he demonstrates clearly what he has learned the next time.

Summary

After observing Nathan I believe I can come to some conclusions. Nathan often participates in behavior that is not suitable for ongoing academic activities.

This behavior does not usually disturb the rest of the class. Often his failure to initiate the appropriate response requested by the teacher interferes with his completion of class work. Nathan needs to focus more on instructions to understand his work. Nathan does show an interest in his work by asking questions. Some of the class work proves to be uninteresting to him. I believe that additional help benefits him. I do not believe his failure to comply with instructions is due to shyness. I have had a chance to speak to him alone and he has said to me, "I like school but there are some things I don't get." I have been informed by the teacher that he receives additional help. I believe that it helps.

Cooperating Teacher's Response

You did an excellent job observing and picking up on his behavior. Your comments were well thought out and seem to fit what I have observed. He does get learning disabilities services. He believes there are things he cannot do, so it takes encouragement to get him to try. He is proud when he does something he thought he could not do.

Instructor's Response

You have done a good study of this boy and made some valid responses. Let me make a couple additional comments and raise some questions for you to consider.

You have pointed out his various work avoidance tactics, and also that he often does not fully understand his assignments. Perhaps after giving an assignment, you could have Nathan come to you and explain what he is supposed to do. Then you have clarified for yourself whether he understood, added any necessary input, strengthened his focus of the work by his explanations, and he has offered your direct attention.

Early in the year I would consider having a parent conference to gain further insight into his patterns of work and behavior at home. When parents are aware of your concerns they may be able to see parallels in activities at home and can reinforce what you are doing in the classroom. Unfortunately, this support is not always available, but you also need to know that.

Did you get any insights into his sense of self among his peers? Does he seem to be accepted socially or to his apparent satisfaction? These are important because it is to such concerns that the mind will wander when work should be uppermost.

It was a thoughtful and supportive addition that your cooperating teacher shared his or her response with you.

chapter five
Planning and Teaching a Lesson

This early clinical experience requires you to design a lesson plan and teach it to the entire class. This lesson should not be out of the regular textbook, but should be an extension of the curriculum. This will give you an opportunity to develop your plan using the Madeline Hunter design rather than depending on the "canned lesson" in the teacher's guide. Only in this way will you be able to evaluate your lesson as you present it to the class. Questions for which you will have immediate feedback: Was the lesson too short? Was there too little content? Was there too much content? Was it too complex for the time available or for the level of the students? Were the students motivated? Did you attain your objective? How do you know if your objective was obtained? Did you allow time for summary? If you are concerned about any of these aspects of your lesson, how would you change it if you were to re-teach it?

Most early clinical students encounter two problems in the preparation of their lesson. First, obtaining ideas for a lesson and, second, anticipating problems that may arise when they implement the lesson in the classroom.

Where can you find ideas? First, look around the classroom the first day you are there. What have the children been studying? Your clues will be taken from their regular textbooks, curriculum guides, bulletin boards, science projects, learning center displays, an assembly program, and a variety of other sources. Many times an early clinical student has complained that he or she could not find an idea for a lesson to teach. When visiting the same classroom one could bring back several ideas that merited further study. You may find ideas for a lesson plan by studying the journals: *The Instructor, School Days, Classmates, Teaching K-8, Creative Classroom,* and specialized subject matter journals, *Arithmetic Teacher, Reading Teacher,* or some other teacher source. Once challenged by a group of students to go to the library and find a lesson idea from the periodical section within thirty minutes, the university supervisor came back with three that could be adapted to grades K-6. There is an exciting array of material from which to choose. Your methods classes on campus will also provide you with ideas to try in the classroom. Included in this chapter is a list of ideas for you to explore.

When you have your idea, check it out with your cooperating teacher. If he or she approves, work out your lesson plan; then discuss it with your university supervisor to get suggestions for improvement.

When you are ready, at least on paper, think about your preliminary preparation. You need to be very complete in your list of supplies (refer to Chapter Nine, Media and Office Equipment). You also need to anticipate problems that may arise. Be sure you know where classroom supplies are kept. For example, if everyone is going to need scissors, do you have extras, or do you know where they are for the student who has lost his or hers?

One early clinical student designed a beautiful art lesson for a fourth-grade class. The presentation went well; the students were highly involved and motivated. Then came time for student participation. The students were to make a design using only the three primary colors and black. It was near the end of the school year and, as you may have guessed, most student crayon boxes were missing at least one of the colors. The student teacher recovered sufficiently to have them go to the classroom crayon box (a large assortment of miscellaneous crayons). Then the next problem arose. How do you distinguish blue from black when the wrapper is gone? The university supervisor, who was observing the lesson, came to the rescue by sorting out the crayons into piles so the selection was easier and faster.

Be sure to discuss your needs with your cooperating teacher. For example, if you need the chalkboard be sure your cooperating teacher has not used it for the following day's language lesson. The best preparation is to anticipate, anticipate, anticipate!

Lesson Plan Procedure

An appropriate lesson plan is like selecting the right dessert to balance well with your main course. Also, having your lesson plan well thought out and organized is similar to working from a well-documented recipe when creating a savory entree. The ingredients must be put together in the correct proportions and in a specific order if the end product is to have merit.

Good planning is highly recognized as the underlying strength to successful teaching. Inspiration and spontaneity are spirited, energizing qualities that add high interest to many lessons. But without a solid, functional plan there is no guarantee that effective instruction will automatically occur. You must have a process to guide you in learning to create a plan for instruction that will help children learn, and will let you evaluate their learning success.

Although there are many ways to go about planning a lesson, (Chapter Six, Instructional Approaches) we have chosen the lesson design presented by Madeline Hunter and Doug Russell.[1]

You first need a general content area and a specific topic or focus in that area around which to build your lesson. A lesson in spelling could focus on working with the construction of contractions as a topic on which to develop an instructional lesson. You must then identify what the specific objectives will be

---

Hunter, Madeline and Doug Russell. "Planning for Effective Instruction." *Instructor,* (September, 1977).

and which students can meet these objectives at an easy level, (working with omitting only one letter), or a more difficult level (leaving out more than one letter and/or returning contractions to their original form). On the basis of this information you will set up the appropriate objectives for the lesson.

Hunter and Russell have organized their process around seven basic steps. Depending on the lesson format, you must decide which given steps are appropriate for the particular objective of the lesson you will teach. Some steps may be combined with another and some may be used in a different sequence than presented here, as is deemed most effective.

Although you have thought through the basic content of your lesson and designed your objectives, when you consider the actual lesson plan, you will begin with:

1. Anticipatory Set

In this part of the lesson you are going to use motivating techniques to gain the interest of the students; relate the lesson to the students' past experience; *and inform the students about the purpose of the lesson.*

Example: I will get the students involved right away by doing review problems on the board. I will pick students to come up to the board to do addition and subtraction problems. We will check them together as a class. If there is a wrong answer, we will go through it as a class.

2. Objective

Be specific in writing your objective. *It should state what you want the students to learn.* The more specific your objective, the easier it will be to execute a successful lesson.

Example: The students will be able to write numbers using the place values of tens and ones.

The ensuing five steps of the Hunter and Russell plan are the "heart" of the lesson. Each step is numbered and an example is included.

3. Input

This is the step in which you determine what information the students need to meet your objectives, and also the means by which you will present that information.

Example: First, I will discuss how often we count by tens. (Note that you are pointing out the relevance and usefulness of the knowledge to be learned.) I will ask the children if there is something on their bodies which consists of ten (fingers, toes). Other questions will be how many pennies are in a dime and how many dimes in a dollar.

Then I will put a number on the board which includes tens and ones (56). I will point out the ones column and the tens column. Next I will point out that there are 5 tens and 6 ones which makes the number 56 (repeat with 31).

Next I will write on the board "8 tens and 2 ones = ____." I will explain that the 2 ones go in the ones column and the 8 tens go in the tens column, so the answer is 82 (repeat with 15).

Following the above, I will write "45 = _____ tens and ____ ones." Students will come to the board. I will ask them how many ones and tens are in a particular number. They will then fill in the blanks.

Lastly, I will show bundles of straws. I will count out ten and rubber band them together. Then I will show single straws that I will also count out. Students will come and write the numbers of straws I have shown.

4. Modeling

This step enables the students to *see* an example of an acceptable finished project. (Note that in the example you are demonstrating the correct procedure and verbalizing as you do so.)

Example: I will use bundled straws of ten to demonstrate tens. Single straws will demonstrate ones. I will hold up one bundle to show a group of ten. I will then write "1 ten" on the board. Next, I will hold up 3 single straws to represent 3 ones. I will write "3 ones" on the board. Lastly, I will write the final answer which is 13. I will be talking as I am writing each step. This will be repeated with numbers 45, 92, and 64.

Following the above, the students will come up front. I will give them a certain number of bundles. They will tell how many tens they have in their hand. Then they will be given single straws. The students will tell how many ones they have. The format of "____ tens and ____ ones = ____" will be on the board. The students will write the number in the correct blanks. I will next model the same concept with sugar cubes.

5. Checking for Understanding

This is the time in the lesson to see if the students understand what is being taught. This may be done by asking questions that will elicit a group response or a written response.

Example: For this exercise the students will give me signals. They will put their hands up if they agree, hands down if they disagree, and hands to the side if they are not sure. I will make statements dealing with certain problems. The children are to tell me if they agree, disagree, or are not sure about what I have said.

86 —   I say: "There are 6 ones."
        Signal: hands up.
         I say: "There are 8 tens."
        Signal: hands up.

20 —   I say: "There are 2 tens."
          Signal: hands up.
          I say: "There are 2 ones."
          Signal: hands down.

Next I will take the straws and hold up 4 bundles and 3 singles. I will write on the board 43. I will ask if they agree with this. Their hands should go up. This will be repeated with the numbers 25 and 91.

6. Guided Practice

This is the time in the lesson when you need to circulate among the students or have them participate at the board. The purpose is to be sure each student understands the ideas you have presented. In certain content areas more than one method may be employed.

Example: On the board will be written "____ tens and ____ ones = ____". I will have a student come up front. I will show groups of ten. The student will write the number in the blank for the tens. I will show single straws which will be the ones. The student will write this number in the blank for the ones. I will then ask another student to read it and tell what number it represents. The student will write the number in the blank. This will be repeated three or four more times. If the students get some answers incorrect, we will work through the problems together.

After working on the board the students will turn to page 51 in their math book. We will work on the first two problems together. They will do the remaining problems on their own. I will walk around to be sure they understand the concept of tens and ones. If they are having problems, I will go back to the concrete example and help them work it out.

7. Independent Practice

This is the opportunity for students to practice the new skill with little or no direction from you.

Example: I will set up a learning center in the classroom that will be equipped with a variety of objects, and problems having to do with tens and ones. The students may work here with the new concept during their free time.

8. Closure and Evaluation

Hunter and Russell refer to closure and evaluation in their seven-step plan. The authors think both are important ingredients of the lesson and have included them as the eighth step in the design of your plan.

This is the time for summarizing the lesson and tying up loose ends. Together you and your students will review the lesson material. This would also be a good time to again relate the relevance of the lesson to everyday life.

You might also want to talk about what the next step and assignment might be. At this point, you should evaluate the presentation of the lesson and determine which students will benefit from additional practice.

Now your written planning is done. Check with your cooperating teacher and university supervisor for any supportive input they may have prior to your teaching opportunity.

Though you are encouraged to develop your lesson making use of the steps of the Hunter and Russell outline, realize that it will not always be necessary or appropriate to incorporate every step. In addition, time constraints and attention needs may call for you to end your lesson on a given day, finishing it at a later time.

Finally, a last word of advice, make preparations well in advance. This includes creating and gathering enough materials for carrying out your lesson, possibly rearranging furniture, setting up any equipment (films, movie projector, filmstrips, and projector, etc.) and knowing that the children are equipped with the materials they need.

Lesson Plan Outline

This lesson plan outline will help you remember the steps necessary for your lesson. It also serves as a guide in analyzing a lesson which will be presented by your university supervisor either in person or by the use of a videotape. This lesson plan follows the Hunter and Russell design and makes it possible for you to see how the steps flow together as the lesson progresses.

Subject   Grade   Teacher   Date

1. **Objective(s)**
   Write this objective behaviorally so it can be measured.

2. **Anticipatory Set** (Motivation & Introduction)
   Motivate students in your topic and make them aware of the purpose or objective of this lesson.

3. **Developmental Activities** (both Procedure & Content)
   A. Input
   B. Modeling
   C. Checking for Understanding
   D. Guided Practice
   E. Independent Practice

4. **Closure and Evaluation**
   Bring closure to your lesson. Let the students restate what they learned. Summarize.

5. **Materials Needed and Preliminary Preparation**

Topic Ideas for Lessons

If your classroom experience is not organized to cover consecutive days, you may have difficulty keeping up with the flow of regular content and will want to select a "one-shot" topic. Again you may find other ideas in the resources recommended. This list of ideas also lends itself to an independent lesson.

Many art projects, poetry and/or creative writing projects may be built around these themes.

Seasonal Lessons: Fall

September:	Leaves, apples and their uses, harvest of crops. Better Breakfast Month, Labor Day, Dog Week, Native American Day.
October:	Pumpkins, migration, hibernation (focus for a good science lesson). National Newspaper Week, Child Health Day, Fire Prevention Week, Columbus Day, Halloween.
November:	Children's Book Week, Cat Week, Favorite Author Day, Veterans Day, Thanksgiving.

Seasonal Lessons: Winter

December:	Bill of Rights Day, winter solstice, Hanukkah, Christmas.
January:	Snow, tracking animals, animals in winter. New Year's Day, Chinese New Year, Inauguration Day, Stephen Foster Memorial Day, Martin Luther King Jr.'s Birthday.
February:	Dental Health Week, Groundhog Day, Valentine's Day, Presidents' Day, National Wildlife Week, Leap Year, Black History Month.
March:	Kites, wind, weather. Weights and Measures Week, Luther Burbank Day, first day of spring, Casimir Pulaski Day, St. Patrick's Day, Passover.

Seasonal Lessons: Spring

April:	Flowers, rain. April Fool's Day, National Library Week, Arbor Day, Earth Day, Easter.
May:	May Day, Mother's Day, Memorial Day, Be Kind to Animals Month.
June:	Summer activities. Flag Day, Father's Day, World Environment Day, summer solstice.

Additional ideas to be used at any time:

Recycling

Endangered species

Safe behavior: might include bus, bike, playground, crossing the street, weather related (electrical, tornado).

Telephone use: courtesy, giving and receiving messages, use in an emergency.

Types of poetry
Types of graphs and how they are used
Famous authors
Current events
Library skills
Chain of life
How to care for a pet
Nutrition
Study habits

The following lesson plan examples were submitted by students in their first clinical experience.

Example One: Language Arts Lesson Plans (Grades 3-6)

Anticipatory Set
a. Focus students' attention by asking them about watching T.V. in general and commercials in particular.
b. Ask students about their favorite T.V. commercials. Guide students into a short discussion about the use of descriptive language in commercials and the ways in which commercials persuade us.
c. Ask students what they think makes one commercial more effective or persuasive than another.

Objective
a. The students will be able to write an original descriptive and persuasive commercial for Mr. Z's Pizza.

Input
a. Pizza samples are distributed to each student to "taste test." Students are asked to notice as many things as possible about the pizza while they are eating it.
b. After samples are eaten, students will describe the pizza in as many ways as possible. The ideas are organized on the chalkboard by categories such as smell, taste, looks, and advantages. Students may want to change these categories or use additional categories.

Modeling
a. On the overhead I will place an example of an original commercial I have written for Kraft Macaroni and Cheese and also one for Hubba Bubba Bubble Gum.

Checking for Understanding
a. Drawing from ideas on the board, I will ask students for examples of descriptive or persuasive sentences about Mr. Z's Pizza. (If needed, provide an example such as Mr. Z's Pizza is double cheesy and double delicious.)
b. These sentences are written on the board for reference.

Guided Practice

a. Each student will be asked to write down his or her lead sentence of the commercial.

b. I will circulate throughout the room, conferencing with each student for a short time, providing help when needed.

Independent Practice

a. Students will continue writing commercials independently, drawing from the ideas on the board.

Follow-up activity: My class will have a Mr. Z's Pizza party and share our commercials.

Example Two: Language Arts - Art/Poetry (Grade 1)

Anticipatory Set

a. I will read a poem to the class. The second time I read the poem, the students will repeat each line after me. Then, the students and I will say the poem in unison.

Objective

a. The students will demonstrate an awareness of fall by creating crayon rubbings of fall leaves.

Input

a. We will talk about the poem—what season it is about, what it tells us about fall, and the color of the leaves.

b. We will talk a little about leaves, why they change color, what happens to them after changing color, and what ways they are useful after they fall.

c. We will talk about them in relation to our senses of seeing, smelling, feeling, and hearing.

d. We will use leaves to create a piece of art by doing a rubbing. Explain what is meant by rubbing.

Modeling

a. I will demonstrate to the students how they will make their leaves. (I will have a bag of leaves for the students to use.)

b. Lay the leaf on your desk with the veins facing up. Place your paper on top of the leaf.

c. Take the crayon with the paper removed, lay the crayon on its side, and rub it over the paper covering the leaf until you can see the leaf pattern on your paper.

d. Color the leaf using the four colors. Cut out your finished leaf.

Checking for Understanding

a. I will have each student do one practice leaf and then do three leaves that will be put on the bulletin board.

Guided Practice

a. I will tell the students to get their crayons and scissors out of their desks and begin to distribute the paper and crayons. I will then pick one group at a time to pick their leaves out of the bag.

Independent Practice
a. The students will begin the project.

Closure and Evaluation
a. After the students have finished their three leaves, they will put their names on the back of each and give them to me. I will put them on the bulletin board where they can admire the full effect of their work.

Example Three: Reading Comprehension Lesson Plan (Grades 1 or 2)

Books: *The Song and Dance Man*, by Karen Ackerman
         Now One Foot, Now the Other, by Tomie de Paola

Anticipatory Set
a. I will begin the lesson by asking the students questions about their grandparents. Then I will tell the students that they are going to hear two stories about two different grandfathers. I will explain to them that they must listen to each story very carefully because they will be doing an activity comparing the two grandfathers in the stories.

Objective
a. The students will demonstrate the ability to distinguish similarities and differences.

Input
a. In reading the stories new vocabulary words will be introduced and defined. The students will be asked to find similarities and differences between the two grandfathers.

Modeling
a. A Venn diagram will be used to illustrate the similarities and differences between the two grandfathers.

Checking for Understanding
a. After reading the first story, I will ask the students to tell me what they know about the grandfather. I will write their responses on the board. The same procedure will be used for the second story. Finally, I will write their responses in the Venn diagram to illustrate the characteristics that are the same and those that are different about the grandfathers.

Guided Practice
a. I will ask for volunteers to tell me something that is similar or different about their grandparents.

Independent Practice
a. I will have the students draw a picture of something they love to do with their grandparent. Under the picture I will ask them to write a sentence or two explaining what they are doing.

Example Four: Math - Ordering Numbers/Greater Than or Less Than (Grade 3)

Anticipatory Set

a. Talk about counting numbers and how they have an order like the alphabet.
b. Ask how high they can count.
c. Ask if certain numbers are higher or lower than others.
d. Ask if they can think of reasons why we need to know greater than or less than about numbers.

Objective

a. Students will be able to distinguish between numbers that are greater than or less than other numbers.
b. Students will be able to list numbers from least to greatest and greatest to least.

Input

a. Have them open the book and read silently while I read aloud to them. Ask a few questions about numbers that are higher or greater than the tree, or smaller or less than the tree. Write many examples of "greater than" equations and "less than" equations on the board. Have the students fill in the sign (<, >). After numerous examples, I will continue on. When they have the hang of ordering numbers least to greatest and greatest to least, I will use unifex blocks to aid in this process. After sufficient examples, homework will be assigned.

Modeling

a. I will write many examples on the board. After they understand most of the lesson, I will use unifex blocks. I will have the students read the whole expression such as 8 > 4 (eight is greater than four). For the unifex blocks, if I hold three in one hand and five in the other, the children will say "three is less than five" and "five is greater than three."

Checking for Understanding

a. Besides having them answer the questions I write on the board, I will have a game. It is around-the-world, but to go on, the student must read the expression on the card correctly with the sign. Example of card: 356 ____ 257. For this they need to know what sign goes in the blank and how to read it.

Guided Practice

a. Some of this is done on the board. I will have them start the homework assignment and I will come around to see if each of them is doing the work correctly.

Independent Practice

a. The unfinished homework will have to be done during their free time or at home.

Closure and Evaluation

a. I will go through and have them name the "alligators" (< = less than alligator, > = greater than alligator) again. I will quickly go through ordering numbers. I will ask a few more questions. If they are correct, I will end the lesson.

Example Five: Bookmaking Activity (Grade 5)

Anticipatory Set

a. I will begin the lesson by asking the students if they have ever heard the fairy tales, *The Three Little Pigs* or *The Frog Prince.* I will find out how much they know about the stories (i.e., sequence of events, characters, setting, etc.)

Objective

a. The students will be able to create their own endings to a known fairy tale.

Input

a. I will have a discussion of the steps involved in process writing and bookmaking. I will read, *The True Story of the Three Little Pigs* and *The Frog Prince Continued.*

Modeling

a. I will model, with the cooperating teacher, how we go through the steps in process writing. I will show them the correct and incorrect ways to go about peer conferencing.

Checking for Understanding

a. I will walk around the room to make sure the students are on the right track and see if they have any questions.

Guided Practice and Independent Practice

a. I will have the students choose a fairy tale and decide if they will write a different version or a continuation. Then I will take time with each group and help them with their prewriting, or "sloppy copy," if they need it.

Evaluation

a. After one of their peers or I edit their "sloppy copy," the students will complete their book, and do the illustrations.

Example Six: Social Studies/Maps (Grade 4)

Anticipatory Set

a. I will begin the lesson by asking the students what they already know about maps. I will encompass the following: boundary, border, north, south, east, west, North Pole, South Pole, compass rose, Equator, hemisphere, latitude, longitude, Prime Meridian, grid, estimate, symbol, key, and scale. These elements will be written on the board for reference.

Objective

a. The students will apply their knowledge of map skills in creating an explorer's map.

Input
  a. I will explain to the students that we have observed how maps of areas have been made, and we have read many different kinds of maps. I will reinforce that the students now have the knowledge to create a map of their own.

Modeling
  a. I will distribute a map of an imaginary place. The students and I will label the map with crayons, using ideas from our discussion.

Checking for Understanding
  a. I will circulate throughout the classroom and check to see if the students are labeling the maps correctly.

Guided Practice
  a. I will divide the class into committees of three to a map. The committees will assemble, decide what type of region they wish to map, and secure whatever is necessary from the materials table.
  b. The maps must include a compass, a set of symbols, a key for any symbols, and a guide (if drawing a map to scale).
  c. I will briefly counsel each committee while circulating throughout the room, and provide help as needed.

Independent Practice
  a. The committees will continue developing and coloring their maps, if time permits.

Example Seven: Science - Recycling (Grade 5)

Anticipatory Set
  a. Show items such as a glass bottle, aluminum can, tin can, plastic jug, foil, plastic bags, catalog, newspaper, weeds, a pumpkin, etc.
  b. Ask questions such as, What can you do with all this junk? Is it recyclable? How do I go about recycling? How do I go about composting? Get them involved.

Objective
  a. The students will demonstrate their understanding of recycling by creating slogans.

Input
  a. I will have content of lesson ready to present to the class, but will ask questions as I go. Students will contribute what they already know about the need for recycling and how it operates in their community. Also, I will ask what the students do to contribute to this very vital process.
  b. Discuss the terms recycle, reuse, reduce, and compost as they apply to this process.
  c. Place these as headings (chart style) on chalkboard.
  d. Pass out work sheet.

Modeling
    a. Go over objects listed on work sheet.
    b. Go over which objects can be recycled, reused, reduced, or composted.
    c. Have students list a couple objects under each heading on board.
    d. Making use of these listings to create a slogan.

Checking for Understanding
    a. Go over items listed so far and have students tell me what it is and why it was placed under that particular heading.

Guided Practice
    a. Complete work sheet at seats.
    b. I will walk around and help as needed.

Independent Practice
    a. Working in groups of three, students will create slogans to encourage recycling.
    b. Students will put slogans on poster board and hang them in the hall.

Closure and Evaluation
    a. Share slogans.
    b. The significance of the students' slogans, and their interest in creating them, will demonstrate the effectiveness of their learning.
      whether it will contribute to your goals or have a high priority for you.

chapter six
Instructional Approaches

In the preceding chapter, you were introduced to a lesson plan model designed by Madeline Hunter and Doug Russell. The use of this model is appropriate for your first lesson planning experiences because it is highly structured. It is also broken down into small components, making it easier for you to plan a detailed lesson.

Certain parts of a lesson plan will always be in place, such as the objective. However, you may want to vary the instructional approach according to the subject matter you are presenting, the make-up of your class group, or because one approach is not working.

It is always exciting to try new approaches. Once you feel confident you have mastered certain steps, try out a new design for presenting your lesson. This chapter will explore some possibilities.

First, you need to have a basic outline, or a guide, so that in the beginning you do not forget any steps.

I. OBJECTIVE: What the student will be able to do as a result of the activity.

II. MATERIALS: The things you will need to teach the lesson.

III. LESSON PRESENTATION: This is your opportunity to plan the lesson using one of the alternate models.

IV. GUIDED AND INDEPENDENT PRACTICE.

VI. FEEDBACK AND EVALUATION: How you will determine if the students have reached the objective.

Inductive lessons differ from the direct lesson (Hunter and Russell) in that the students will discover the concept, generalization, or definition without you presenting it to them. The following is an inductive lesson using the concept development model.

This lesson is designed for a first-grade classroom:

OBJECTIVE:
The students will develop an understanding of why we celebrate Veterans Day.

MATERIALS:
Chalkboard, chalk, writing paper, construction paper.

LESSON PRESENTATION:

1. Making the list: Ask the students to "tell me everything you know about Veterans Day." Accept everything the students say at this point. Some of the responses might be:

about war	holiday	men
they are dead	no school	brave
my uncle's one	flags fly	guns

2. Grouping the items: "Which of these items might go together? Why?"

   Example: Tom's uncle
   men

3.   Labeling, defining relationship: "What would you call the groups you have formed?"

   Example: PEOPLE
   Tom's uncle
   men

4.   Regrouping, reanalyzing: "Are there items in one group that you could put with another group? Do you want to add or subtract any items? Do you want to add another group?"

   Example: PEOPLE
   Tom's uncle
   men
   women (added)

5. Summarizing the data, making generalizations: "Can you give me a sentence about all of these groups?"

   The sentences at this point will help you evaluate the students' understanding of why we celebrate Veterans Day. While you would record the sentence, "A day when we fly flags," as a response, you might have the students decide if this sentence or the following, "We remember men and women who fought for our country," is a better statement.

FEEDBACK AND EVALUATION:

You have been evaluating this lesson during the entire process and by the poem which becomes the end product.

Further activities in the learning center for the week would include illustrating the sentences from the lesson. These sentences would be printed on sentence strips, and paper would be available for the picture.

Another type of inductive lesson is the inquiry lesson. Any subject will lend itself to inquiry since the process begins with a puzzling situation and ends with finding a reasonable solution.

This example of an inquiry lesson is designed for second grade:

OBJECTIVE:

The students will be able to identify the elements necessary for plant growth.

MATERIALS:

Chalkboard, chalk, plants (two that have been growing in the classroom), and additional ones for the students.

LESSON PRESENTATION:

1. The problem: Two plants received the same amount of water, are planted in similar soil, and were transplanted when they were the same size. "Why is one so much larger than the other?"

2. Introduce the process to the class: Students may ask only questions that can be answered "Yes" or "No." They must wait to be called on. They cannot discuss the problem with their classmates.

3. Gather data: Students ask, "Are they the same kind of plant." "Yes." "Did you measure the water?" "Yes." "Did you keep one in the closet?" "No." "Were they in different parts of the room?" "Yes." "Was one closer to the window?" "Yes."

4. Develop a theory: Once the students have determined it is a matter of light, this may go on the board as an accepted theory. The students may also elect to discuss it among themselves or ask more questions.

5. State the rule: Plants need sunlight in order to grow strong and healthy.

6. Analyze the process: How did you put cause and effect together?

GUIDED PRACTICE:

Students suggest other problems they want to investigate: "Would classroom lights work? Would fluorescent lights be better? Do all types of plants require the same amount of light?" Divide the class into groups by which questions they want to work on. Assist them in setting up their experiments.

EVALUATION:

Observation during the lesson, also as the experiments are being developed. Each research team will present the results of their experiments on sentence charts at completion of the project with a summary of what was learned.

Certain lesson approaches or models may be classified as social models. Role playing and simulation are among these and are often used as a learning tool. Another successful social model is the use of cooperative learning groups. Cooperative learning may be as simple as having two students pair off to give each other a spelling test. In other instances, the groups are larger and encompass a greater degree of subject matter.

Most student teachers and beginning teachers tend to overlook the positives of cooperative learning because they fear the class will get out of control. This may be minimized by setting behavior standards for students who are working in groups.

The lesson that is presented here is for a third-grade class of mixed abilities:

OBJECTIVE:

Students will be able to write an ending to a story while working as a team.

MATERIALS:
Unfinished stories, paper, pencil, vocabulary lists, (if needed), heterogeneous group list, and designated roles.*

LESSON PRESENTATION:
Explain to the students that they will be divided into study teams, each with four members. Each member will be assigned a responsibility. Together they are to come up with an ending to the story that they will be given. When they have agreed on an ending, they are to record it and have everyone in the team sign it.

Establish the behavior for the team.
1. No student leaves the group until the assignment is completed.
2. Each team member is responsible for seeing that the assignment is completed.
3. If a student has difficulty with any part of the assignment, they consult the team before going to the teacher.
4. Students must work quietly so they do not disrupt the others.

Assemble the teams according to the list. If random groups are desired, you would simply count off by fours.

Pass out stories to each team as soon as the students are in place. In this lesson the key roles would be as follows: Give each student a card with his or her role printed on it.

Example:　　Mary — reader (reads the unfinished story)
　　　　　　　Tim — recorder (records the ending)
　　　　　　　Jane — motivator (makes sure everyone participates)
　　　　　　　Jim — encourager (encourages each idea)

Study teams begin to work on their endings. You circulate to see that the process is working, noting students who are having problems with the process, and assisting where needed.

GUIDED PRACTICE:
In the group itself.

EVALUATION:
The finished product (ending) for the story will be presented by each group to the class. You will also need to evaluate the effectiveness of each group as a cooperative team and decide how well the students handled their individual roles.

---

* Note: As a student teacher you might need help in forming the groups. Since the teams should be balanced in terms of ability, motivation, and gender, your cooperating teacher's knowledge of the classroom may be necessary. Also, some explanation of the role of each team member should precede the lesson.

A student teacher may see a cooperative lesson as a very ambitious endeavor and be rather disappointed with the results. Certain factors must be considered in each situation. Have the students engaged in any type of group work or is this a classroom where all of the lessons are highly structured? Were the groupings by abilities and personalities appropriate? Again, as with many of your lessons, and regardless of how it is presented, this is a learning experience. If you are open to learn more about these processes firsthand, this is the time. Your cooperating teacher and your university supervisor will help you over the rough spots. Or, better yet, ask your cooperating teacher to model the process for you.

In this chapter, several lesson designs have been presented. The inductive model using the concept application, the inquiry model, and a social model such as the cooperative group. The model presents the steps to follow to arrive at a desired outcome.

The method you select should depend on what the students are expected to learn. Just as you would not choose a recipe for meat loaf when you want to produce a dessert, you cannot expect a model designed to bring about recall of facts to produce divergent thinking.

Suggested References:

Gunter, Mary Alice, Thomas Estes, and Jan Schwab. "Instruction, A Models Approach." Boston, Allyn and Bacon, 1990.

Pasch, Marvin, Georgia Sparks-Langer, Trevor Gardner, Alane Starko, and Christella Moody. "Teaching as Decision Making." New York, Longman, 1991.

chapter seven
Bulletin Boards

This clinical experience requires that you create and put up a bulletin board appropriate for the classroom to which you are assigned. Bulletin boards are traditionally a part of the elementary school classroom. They may be used to relay information, keep track of days and holidays, display children's work, call attention to special events, or to decorate the room. And whatever their purpose, they should be kept current and relevant.

For the student teacher, two problems may arise: First, where to find an idea and, second, how to implement that idea. Again the teachers' magazines will have many excellent ideas. The *Instructor* has a section on bulletin boards in each issue, and many magazines have bulletin board ideas to correlate with a unit or a single lesson plan. In Appendix E, you will find a list of resources that will prove very helpful to the beginning teacher.

If you do not consider yourself artistic, the problem of creating the bulletin board may cause some concern. This lack of ability can be easily solved. Now is the time to start collecting patterns for future bulletin boards. Besides the many books with patterns included, there are several other sources. Coloring books are available on almost every subject and often feature the current fads, such as Teenage Mutant Ninja Turtles. Some of the old standbys—Peanuts, Smurfs, and Garfield—are always popular with the elementary school student. Greeting cards, newspaper advertisements, napkins, and wrapping paper are other sources you should add to your collection. One newspaper advertisement on "Back to School Values" featured a large group of children and a school bus, and served as a pattern for a welcome-back bulletin board. It also covered nutrition (one of the children was carrying an apple) and school bus safety.

Your pattern may be enlarged by placing it under the opaque projector and focusing it on paper taped to the wall. (Because the opaque is such a good teaching aid, it is standard equipment in most elementary schools.)

You may also run the pattern through the thermofax and make a transparency to project on the wall with the overhead. If you want to combine your bulletin board character with a student worksheet, you should make a ditto master at the same time.

Many of the schools in which you will work will have large rolls of colored paper (sometimes referred to as butcher paper) available for covering the bulletin board. If this is unavailable, you may cover your boards with wallpaper, burlap,

Figure 7-1 Seasonal

maps, newspaper, fabric, paper, plastic tablecloths, or gift wrap. The possibilities are endless. All boards look more complete when you add a border. You may want to cut one from paper, use paper chains, paper plates, adding machine paper with printed designs, or seasonal shapes. Some of the books listed in the

Figure 7-2 Student Work

resource section specialize in a variety of ideas for borders. Avoid making the border so busy that it detracts from your bulletin board's focus.

Lettering for your bulletin board will be much easier if you make or buy a set of letters that are reuseable. Some technology laboratories or learning

Figure 7-3 Subject Matter

centers have letter-making machines available for your use.

You should take advantage of your clinical experience and take pictures or make sketches of bulletin boards you might use in the future. This does not need to be restricted to the classroom to which you are assigned.

Figure 7-4 Student Participation

Bulletin boards will gradually become less ominous as you get more involved with them. They are not the total focus of teaching and should not consume a great part of your planning time. But they do add a great deal to learning and contribute to an appealing classroom environment.

chapter eight
Games and
Learning Centers

This clinical experience requires you to create an educational game appropriate for the academic content of the grade level to which you are assigned. It is good to make yourself aware of the present skills and content being studied in your classroom, and then work to develop a game that would reinforce this learning.

You may think of games as play activities and question what place they have in an educational setting. Games encompass many values important to the developmental growth of children. While having fun and engaging in learning, the children are given constructive social interaction.

Classroom teachers use games with children for motivation and to reinforce newly learned skills. Games enhance the instructional program and provide a review of skills and subject content.

Providing learning through the use of games creates a legitimate vehicle for children to meet developing social behaviors. The grasping of a newly learned skill by an insecure child is positive reinforcement, and builds confidence when accompanied by peer support in a small group setting. Children need social contact aside from the limits of recess and the confines of a highly structured classroom.

Utilizing games in the classroom develops greater independence, better organization, and stronger work study skills in students. They learn to work well in their seats to earn the privilege of game playing, and then must conduct themselves appropriately if they are to maintain the privilege.

It takes thoughtful organization on the part of the teacher to appropriately group and assign children to the games. You quickly learn combinations of girls and boys who can work well together, who finish their assignments in about the same time, and those who make good peer helpers. A chart with pockets labeled with names can be used to assign games to those needing reinforcement of a specific skill.

When handled well by the classroom teacher, children learn to cooperate, to share, and to be patient and supportive to those giving slower responses. They also learn to be responsible if it is their turn to be the group leader for the day or week, to be a good listener when it is not their turn to be the leader, to win or lose with grace, and to accept all classmates into their group.

Once you gradually pattern both the children and yourself into the daily routine and rules of the classroom, games can be a real asset to you and a benefit to the children. As they learn to organize and fill their time with assignments, followed by appropriate available independent learning activities, you will receive fewer interruptions as you work with small groups, and will have the assurance that they are using their time constructively.

Learning centers or stations, though not classified as games, are mentioned here since they have many of the same attributes as games and compliment the use of games. They foster good independent mobility and use of time within the learning situation. A learning center, like a game, focuses on one area of learning or a particular skill. For example, a station could be set up with activities that change every week and center on the use of a dictionary, on poetry, how to use a telephone book, letter writing, compound words, or contractions. Children would be assigned to these individually, either by a special interest such as a challenge level activity, or by the need for reinforcement. While most games involve two to four children, the learning centers essentially involve one person; though it is conceivable that you could develop project-type activities that would engage more than one child.

Are you wondering how you can do all of this? What about the noise level? Who creates all this material? These are good questions. First, you charge up your enthusiasm and develop your strategy. Go ahead and dream. It may not all come true but you will work at it. Start simple and keep it growing. You do not walk in on Monday morning with fifteen learning centers and twenty new games. It would be very difficult to come up with that much all at once, and the children could never digest it all. They need gradual immersion into the total process of having games and/or learning centers as an integral part of their learning process. As you see a need to develop a specific learning skill, you create the tool—a new game or two, perhaps a learning center to enhance your teaching and the children's interest in learning. Gradually you add to your treasures as need and enthusiasm motivate.

If you find noise or over zealousness a problem, look at the causes and pursue possible remedies. Perhaps you need to look at your room arrangement. This is an important factor that will be discussed in Chapter Ten (Classroom Organization). Set up rules—few and direct—that must be followed. Communicate what is an acceptable noise level with consideration to fellow classmates, what constitutes the need to return to their seat, and be prepared to act on it. Consistency with children is extremely important. Be aware that there is a difference between noise and constructive noise. The latter is far better than a dull, quiet classroom.

Look at who creates these games and materials you would like to use with your students. Take a look around you. What resources are available to you in your community? If there is a good teacher store in commuting distance, you may wish to browse and pick up a book or two of games appropriate to the needs of your class. There is a partial list of references in Chapter Twenty-One (School Supply Stores), Appendix F (Games), and Appendix G (Learning Centers).

Once you have decided on some games you would like to have, get the necessary materials. Summers are a good time to add items to your educational learning activities. Ask parents for assistance. A table in your classroom or the hall stocked with supplies and directions where parents can work and socialize will reap a harvest of activities for your students. In some areas you can find volunteer grandparents to do the same. Give it some publicity with a photograph and an article in your local newspaper.

The whole process of game-making can be made easier by accumulating materials and keeping them together for easy accessibility. A large basket or heavy cardboard box would be handy. You could collect orange juice or soup cans to use as compartments for organizing supplies while keeping them readily accessible. Some materials you might want to include in your supply basket are:

crayons

water base markers—both fine and wide

permanent markers—not to be used under lamination as they will bleed

rubber cement

white glue or glue stick

scissors

razor blades

paper clips

rubber bands

scotch tape

pencils

paper punch

decorative stickers—make good game board markers

tissue paper

zip lock bags—hold game pieces

yarn—various colors

index cards—white or colored

brass paper fasteners

dice

plastic discs or buttons—game markers

spinners

wooden cubes—good for dice (can put large numbers on them for adding or subtracting games)

clear contact—for use on items that will not go through a laminator

Various colors of tagboard should be available to you in your school and can be cemented to heavier cardboard. Other types of board that can be purchased where art supplies are sold include index board and railroad board.

Old workbooks and some coloring books are good sources for pictures. And for enlarging a picture, remember to use the opaque projector. It is easy to operate and gives you quick enlargements.

Use local sources to obtain useful items. Styrofoam meat trays from the local butcher, pizza boards from the pizzeria, old wallpaper sample books from the decorator shop, or large ice cream tubs from the ice cream parlor are useful items.

Be sure that your games are created from durable material. And, once created, have them laminated so they will hold up over time. If your school does not have a laminating machine, see if there is a petty cash fund available or if the PTA would contribute.

References here have been essentially to games of a language arts nature. It is not intended to limit ideas to this subject area. Math games are vital to skill learning and many find social studies and science games highly useful, especially at the intermediate level. However, at the kindergarten and primary levels it is natural to focus on language and math skills.

There are games for one person only, others for two, three or four players, and some that are good to use with the entire class. It is not often you have a skill reinforcement need that applies to the entire group, so you will tend to develop small group activities.

Take a look at commercial games and you may find an idea that can be adapted to your classroom needs. Battleship™ gives the children a greater concept of coordinate geometry. You need to put tape across the bottom row of the game board and down the left hand side. Then number each tape from zero to ten to represent the positive quadrant. Dominoes is another good game to use and gives the children some addition practice.

And here is another good use of parent help, especially in math games. Many games you will use daily and they will go well independently, but there are others that need adult supervision as rules are explained and learned. Perhaps you might spend a portion of a math class once each week with two or three parents assigned to supervise small groups and guide them through learning the rules. After six or eight weeks of rotating children from group to group, you will find the children capable of functioning on their own. At this time you may decide to introduce some new games or to use the parents in some other venture.

As you proceed, both your ideas and your enthusiasm will grow. The possibilities are endless. Begin now to gather ideas by taking photos and by writing descriptions and rules onto index cards to file for future reference.

Following are a few ideas for game activities. You will find many uses for items that you would typically toss in the garbage. A milk carton is used here to create a carton computer.

I. Materials Needed:
    a. half-gallon milk carton
    b. one sheet index board

     c. your choice of covering for the carton such as:
        1. contact paper
        2. wall paper
        3. wrapping paper
     d. glue or rubber cement
     e. scissors
     f. ruler

II. Directions:
     a. Open carton top so you can reach inside.
     b. Cut two slits, 2 1/2" x 1" in front of carton. (See Diagram 1)
     c. Cut two strips of index board
        1. one 3 3/4" x 10 1/2"
        2. one 3 3/4" x 8"
     d. Fold each end of each strip over about 3/4" and cut for tabs.

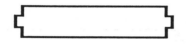

     e. Either glue or tape strips inside the carton (see Diagram 2) being sure to do the bottom of the longer strips first, the shorter or inside strip next, and the top of the longer strip last. (Inside of carton with tabs affixed to outside.)

     f. While carton is still open decorate the outside as you desire. Use any material of your choice (some suggested under Materials Needed). If students are making computers individually as a class project you may wish to have them use plain paper they can decorate by gluing various junk items (buttons, yarn, old beads, bottle caps, spools, etc.) onto them.
     g. Make skill cards 1 1/2" x 2 1/2". Place the skill on the front, flip card over top to bottom so when you place the answer on the back it will be upside down from how the skill was placed on the front.
     h. Laminate the cards and notch upper right corner for easy sorting.

The following skill areas lend themselves to the carton computer format:

Math	Reading
counting	vowel sounds
number words	beginning consonant sounds
addition facts	alphabetizing
subtraction facts	color words
multiplication facts	contractions
division facts	synonyms
fractions	antonyms
telling time	homophones
money	

The triangle board is another educational game. It can be large or small and is made from three pieces of sturdy board. Railroad board is good for this. Cut three pieces the same size, approximately 10" x 24". They may be covered with clear contact paper or laminated for durability. Tape them together with wide plastic tape.

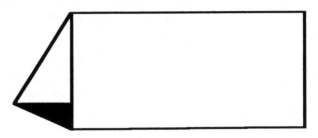

Possible uses:

1. By using masking tape, colored clips or clothespins, this triangle board can be used as a display stand for interesting items, challenging thoughts for the day, learning centers, and student work. By standing the triangle on end, all three sides can be used.

2. Set triangle board on its side and place metal rings (key rings of various sizes) into both pieces of board at the top of the triangle. Make cards, mark as desired, and punch a hole in the top.

   a. Word Flip: write single letters or combinations on each card. Place on appropriate rings. Children then flip cards to make words.

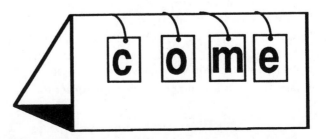

b. Sound Match: one set of cards will have initial consonant, blend, or diagraph cards. The other rings will have picture cards. Students will match appropriate pictures to correct beginning sounds.

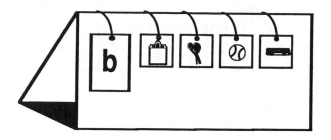

3. Make it into a board with adhesive-backed hangers attached to the surface. Make playing cards from index board, laminate, and punch with a hole for hanging. Words can be hung on appropriate hooks for matching and classifying in a variety of ways: beginning sounds, short vowels, long vowels, how many syllables, singular or plural, etc.

   a. Picture-Word Match—Vocabulary Development: Picture cards are made for various parts of speech in specific categories: nouns, action words, adjectives, seasonal, transportation, etc. Corresponding word cards are made by writing the word on a small piece of index board and covering it with two pieces of clear adhesive-backed plastic the same size as the picture cards. In this way, the picture will be seen after the word card is hung on the correct picture. The students hang up all the picture cards and then place the correct word card over each picture.

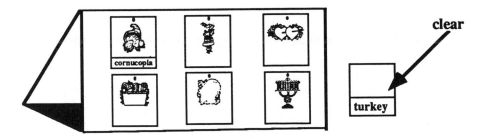

   b. Build a Word Board: Six to eight hooks are attached to the board. Letter cards are made by consonants, blends, diagraphs, vowels, endings, etc. The cards are placed into containers by classification. The students find the correct letters for the desired word. This could be an alternate method of practicing spelling words.

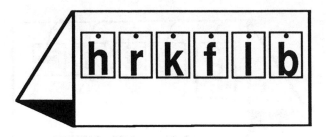

Scan the list of materials listed in the appendixes, and visit a teacher store, your library, and any other resources available to you. As you gather ideas and useful materials you will find it invigorating and contagious.

chapter nine
Media and Office Equipment

Prior to your classroom experience, you need to become familiar with both audio-visual and office equipment. Most colleges offer courses that will give you the opportunity to operate these machines and instruction in producing learning aids. The learning centers of most libraries are also equipped with these machines, and their staff is available to assist you in their operation.

The audio-visual equipment should include: movie projector (self-threading and manual), filmstrip projector, overhead projector, opaque projector (a rarity in many college classrooms, but an essential part of many elementary schools), VCR, record player, tape recorder (reel and cassette), and laminator.

Office equipment should include: ditto machine, copying machine, thermofax (for making dittos and transparencies), and a basic computer.

Knowledge of these will give you increased confidence as you face your first classroom experience. Since different brands of equipment may require different operating methods, it is to your advantage to check on the equipment in your particular school. Both your cooperating teacher and the office staff will answer your questions and assist you. If you are unsure of how to use the equipment, ask!

The use of the appropriate equipment will not only enhance your lesson but will also be a valuable tool in producing bulletin boards, games, etc.

chapter ten
Classroom Organization

Recently a Chicago principal said, the teachers in his school indicated their second biggest problem behind discipline was coping with all the paperwork. This remark was given support by a National Education Association (NEA) survey in 1985, in which 92 percent of the teachers reported they loved to teach, but spend too much time on paperwork and administrative tasks. Few of you have chosen to become teachers because you enjoy writing reports, correcting papers, and answering memos from the office. If you want to spend quality time teaching children, it is imperative that you learn good organization and time-management skills.

There is no better time than the present. Your first clinical experience, as well as the others that follow, will give you the opportunity to observe the management skills of other classroom teachers. You will also need to reflect on how you would do it differently. Ask questions to learn firsthand how various teachers organize their rooms and materials. Be aware of anything that seems to detract from the room's appearance. For example, avoid being the pack-rat teacher who keeps everything and has it stored on shelves, in cupboards, and in boxes all over the room, while most of it is fairly inaccessible for quick use. These individuals will have a less attractive room for the children, less space for their own use, and unwanted materials. Too much time will be wasted locating what you need. Work toward an uncluttered environment. It will be easier for you to efficiently make use of appropriate materials and create a more pleasant classroom for the children. If you want them to develop strong work study skills and good housekeeping habits, it must begin with you.

In addition, this is the time for you to begin collecting not only ideas but also materials. In doing so, carry your camera, take pictures of outstanding bulletin boards throughout the building, make note cards of specific lessons, art projects, poems, and other items that warrant saving, collect patterns, and begin your own file. Think about how you wish to set up your filing system. Many seasonal items are most efficiently filed by the month—when you sit down each August to plan for September you only need to pull your month's file. There, you will find bulletin board ideas, seasonal work sheets, art projects, poetry, a list of good stories, and creative writing ideas relative to that time. Much of your basic content materials will be best filed under content headings since their use will be governed by the readiness of your students. Another dimension of filing is that if you subscribe to any teacher publications, you will naturally want to read and use them while they are current. You might find it helpful in the long run to cut out only what you want to save and file it immediately. That charming poem on Halloween ghosts will elude you next year when you want it unless it is already in your October file. You will not use everything again, but you can add or discard. Be selective. And you have eliminated the messy stack of saved magazines to take from your valuable time later down the road. The sooner you come up with an organizational system, the better off you will be.

Take a typical beginning to any classroom day. The bell rings and the day is about to begin. The children file into the classroom. You have three administrative tasks that must be handled immediately: take attendance, find out who is eating hot lunch (possibly collect lunch money if it is the beginning of the week), and salute the flag. On this particular day, Mary has brought twenty-five cupcakes for a birthday treat later in the day; Joey and Bobby have been fighting before school and the playground supervisor waits with the report; and you notice that Sam, who has very low self-esteem, looks even more unhappy than usual.

Your conflict results from what you as a caring teacher want to do and what the administrative responsibilities demand. You realize that to set an up-lifting tone for the day you need to wish Mary a "happy birthday" and get out the birthday chair for her, get to the cause of the fight between Joey and Bobby so they are ready to start the day, and find time to give Sam a special smile, hug, or whatever seems appropriate. On the other hand, you dare not risk the secretary's displeasure by being late with the lunch count or forgetting the attendance until after lunch.

What are some of the ways you might resolve the problem? First, you might share some of the responsibility with the students. Taking attendance and lunch count is much easier if each student takes a colored tag from a box and hangs it on his or her peg (the tags may be colored so that red indicates hot lunch, green is cold lunch, etc.). At the end of the day one of the students is assigned to place the tags back in the box. Appoint a classroom monitor to begin the pledge to the flag (even the youngest student can be responsible for this). In one extremely well-organized classroom, the children stood at attention and saluted the flag as soon as the final bell had rung.

Second, you might want to enlist the help of a student from another classroom to take attendance and lunch count, especially if this is a primary grade. These same students might be used at other times during the day to assist with an art lesson, because you must always be in the room. Another valuable and too often untapped source of volunteer help is parents and senior citizens. This was mentioned in Chapter Seven.

Third, start the day with a brief assignment you have written on the board or the overhead so each student has something to do when they walk in. Some teachers set the timer and give five minutes to sharpen pencils, select a library book, finish writing in their journals, or whatever task is appropriate. But be aware of a good balance between structure toward getting the group started in an organized way, while allowing for social interchanges among peers, and between the students and you. They often have much to relate and will settle in better if they have had adequate opportunity to share a moment with you.

The best teachers are well organized. While you may know a creative teacher who has not seen the top of her desk since the beginning of the school year and pays little attention to routine matters of classroom management, for most, getting organized pays big dividends.

As a student teacher you will need a complete class list with students' addresses and phone numbers. Be sure to make several copies so you can have one at home. When you become a teacher, you will find it very helpful to keep one in the classroom, one in your office mailbox and one at home. This way the phone numbers you need are always at hand.

Most cooperating teachers will also see that you have a current seating chart so you can begin to learn the students' names. Part of the organization of any classroom is the arrangement of desks and activity areas. Again, the challenge for you is to rearrange the room (in your mind) in other patterns. Desks in rows seem to be the norm in many classrooms, but be imaginative as to how they might serve the needs of the students. Chart these ideas for future reference so as a teacher you will have a variety of seating plans you believe will work. Organizing a classroom is a very personal thing and there are many needs to consider. As a student teacher be aware of the classroom to which you are assigned and to other rooms in your building. The room arrangement should be appealing and pleasant to one entering the room and functional for your teaching style. In some respects it can be likened to decorating your home. Bare walls and furniture can be stark and unfriendly, but adding appropriate touches for attractive balance, making interesting groupings, and adding items of interest, such as plants, an aquarium, children's art work, and pillows or a rocker in the reading corner, can transform your room into a happy, comfortable place in which to work and play. It makes a statement about you and how you incorporate the children into this special environment for learning.

Many teachers still adhere to the norm of putting desks in rows facing the board. This may have some merit on occasion, but it ignores the needs of children to work in social groupings. This is an important developmental need. It also causes more disruption when you need to group desks for special projects and peer teaching. If desks are already placed in groups of four, for example, creating a table, you can always move individuals into various combinations by having the children move. This avoids a total furniture rearrangement, which can cause disruption. If you expect the best from children, they will tend to give you their best and will quickly settle into working quietly in small groups. And you will also learn which combinations of children are more positive and supportive.

A second-grade girl, Ann, complained that she could not get her work done because she was disturbed by the boy sitting beside her. When asked by her teacher if she had communicated her needs to Bobby, she said she had not. The teacher then suggested that Ann relate her concerns to Bobby. Bobby appeared to be surprised by the message from Ann. The teacher asked him if he realized he was creating a problem for Ann. Bobby was also asked what he could do about it, and if he thought that by observing the way Ann went about her work that it might help him learn to give more attention to how he got his work done. Bobby was quick to admit that it would probably help him to at least try. Ann proved to be a positive influence on Bobby. She learned to go directly to the source of the problem and gained some self confidence as she felt needed by Bobby rather than just seeing him as her tormentor.

There will always be some distractions no matter how you seat children. But it is better to consider their needs for social groupings, and give them the rules for making it work, than being arbitrary and have them fulfill their social needs in devious ways.

It is often the practice to put the more disruptive individuals toward the back of the room where they will not bother the others so much. More often than not, bad behavior is a negative call for attention. By placing them farther away, they add rejection to their sense of need. Children need our acceptance and approval on a daily basis, and rows tend to create a pecking order. You may be one who feels rows are good, but if you encounter behavior problems, though they may not be caused by this arrangement, give consideration to this possibility.

Creating areas in your room can add interest to the arrangement. Try several combinations to find one that works best for you and the group with which you are working. Large rooms naturally give you greater possibilities. By placing the reading table in the center of the room (round ones are nice because everyone is equally near you), you are at the hub, and the children work more quietly sensing your nearness. It is true that your back will be to the children, but you must have some trust. Children need closeness and you are not a paper doll. Desks may be grouped in twos or fours a bit apart from the reading table. Then the wall areas are free for interest centers and activities. Some activities may need wall outlets—such as tape recorders, individual film strip projectors, record players, or computers.

What are other ideas you need to consider? Following are a few suggestions to help you organize and work efficiently while giving consideration to your needs as a teacher.

1. You will be a more effective teacher if you take some time for yourself. The days of the spinster teacher who arrived at 6 a.m., corrected papers at recess and lunch, and left the building at 5 p.m. are over. Be good to yourself. Take some time to get away during your break. You may want to have a "care" package just for you in your classroom. Fix a cup of herbal tea, put up your feet, read an interesting article, and refresh yourself. You will be a better teacher for it.

2. Be sure your desk or table is conducive to spreading out your work. Enlarge your work area if necessary.

3. Be sure you have an extra sweater for those days when you have recess duty and the weather report is inaccurate.

4. Work out a filing system that will best serve your needs. A dual system—by the month for seasonal and thematic material, and by content for subject matter material—has already been suggested. Then you have your daily and weekly plans to keep efficiently organized: those that deal directly with the students, and those that have to do with your professional matters. To manage your classroom daily lessons, label five folders, one for each day of the week,

and a sixth one for the following week. As a student teacher, this will help you keep tabs on the classroom to which you are assigned (even when you are not there) and it is good practice for when you have your own classroom. It will serve you best as an accommodation for reports for the principal, curriculum committee, etc. Complete and file the report under the day it is due.

5. Color coding may be used in several ways to simplify your life. One teacher developed a math file for use in a first-grade classroom by using a variety of colored file cards. These cards, filed under the appropriate skill, were easy to identify by the code on the cover: white—game idea; pink—finger play; yellow—student activity; green—filmstrips or book; and blue—manipulatives to order. This type of organization made it easier to fill out a "wish" list when the principal requested it. The blue cards included the proper catalogues, prices, page numbers, etc., so filling out the order was greatly simplified. Color coding will also help students know where to return classroom materials, how to locate game or puzzle pieces, and identify easy-to-read books from the more difficult. You may want to color code the students' file by placing a red circle on the file of a student with a medical problem (needs to wear glasses daily) or blue on one that contains a letter requesting no corporal punishment. The uses of color coding are limited only by your imagination.

6. When filing, organize your teaching materials by topics, skills, and new ideas. If you are teaching a unit on weather, keep all your materials on that subject together, including a list of materials you may want to order for next year. The list will assist you when it is time to order new materials. Formulate a system for recording them or color coding them as you go.

7. In the primary grades, when children are using disposable workbooks, it is often more efficient to tear pages out as units, collate them, and cross stack them for use. This eliminates your searching for the right page to correct, messy tear-outs and dog-eared pages. This is also a good way to make use of parent volunteers.

8. Make permanent folders for children's weekly work to be filed as you grade it. These can be filed by children, as appropriate, or with volunteer help. You can use file folders with students' names on them, perhaps decorated by the children, and laminated. Have a sheet inside for the parent to sign, indicating that he or she has received it, and reviewed the child's work for the week. As the folders are returned Monday morning, one of the children can place them in the correct file box in alphabetical order. This is good practice.

9. Keep materials where they are to be used. A rolling cart or a large dish pan may be used to keep a group of reading workbooks near the reading circle and not cluttering up your desk. Having duplicates (staplers, for example) in more than one area will also be helpful.

10. Use baskets, contact paper-covered boxes, or plastic dish pans for children to place their finished work and another one for them to put *un*finished work. This makes it easier for you to know who needs to be followed up on. A flat

shelf or table where students can stack their finished workbooks, open to the page that needs correction, will save you time when grading. And letting children turn in work as they complete it helps them clear off their work spaces while allowing them legitimate mobility within the classroom setting.

11. How do you plan to handle bathroom breaks? Unless mandated by school rules, try to develop a policy that avoids lining up the whole class and having to keep students quiet in the halls. Develop a process that does not interrupt you as you teach—perhaps a red/green signal by the door. When it is red, students know someone is out and they must wait their turn. A green signal means they can go—one at a time. Watch for students making several trips to the bathroom every couple of hours. By checking to see if the student has a problem, you also make him or her aware you know what is going on. It works very well.

12. How do you plan to handle sharpening pencils, putting away materials, and checking out library books? To the novice teacher, students going to the pencil sharpener to sharpen a broken pencil makes good sense. It is only after the teacher has observed the epidemic of broken pencils, the tendency to poke another student with the sharp tip, and the social grouping around the pencil sharpener that changes are made. There are several solutions: sharpened pencils on the teacher's desk that students may use; a pencil bulletin board where you may also borrow one; and sharpening several pencils at a time.

Good organization also involves anticipating problems that may arise in the daily routine. You may observe the cooperating teacher's solution to these problems, but you also need to think through your own. How do you plan to handle each of these concerns? What method will you use? A well-organized classroom teacher will have anticipated these situations so they do not become problems. A well-planned classroom will eliminate many discipline problems.

chapter eleven
Time Management

Time management is more difficult than organizing the classroom and materials. The elementary classroom teacher must be fully prepared before the students' day begins. Therefore, time management becomes an essential skill. During your clinical experience you will experience the frustration of too little time. Juggling your first clinical experience with your other class responsibilities will not be easy, but it can be done. With all of these demands on your time it is imperative that you set priorities.

Why is it that so many of us feel powerless over our time? One reason is that definite goals have not been established. Without definite plans it is hard to stay on the right road. You may know what you want to do, but believe there are too many obstacles in your way. This is especially true while you are a student. However, there are some things you *can* do.

First, identify your major goals. In Appendix H, there is an open-ended sentence exercise. Take the time to fill it out. Look at it again later and identify at least three major goals in your academic life and in your social life (you may add community service life also, if appropriate). Write them down and put them somewhere: on your mirror, by your desk, wherever you will see them every day. Next to the telephone is often the best place. You will be amazed at how many times your decision-making is done on the phone.

Second, make appropriate decisions with your goals in mind. One of the author's major goals was to improve the lives of the seriously mentally ill. When asked to serve on the state Board of the Alliance for the Mentally Ill, the response was a quick "yes" because it had a direct bearing on her goal. This was a time-consuming commitment, but because she set priorities, the time was available.

Third, take a step in the right direction, no matter how small. Divide your goal into smaller objectives. Then, even if time and money are constraints, you can still begin its implementation. Take, for example, learning to fly. Some preliminary steps would be to visit the pilots' lounge and talk with other pilots, check out books and videos on learning to fly, join the Civil Air Patrol, and fly as an observer with a pilot. Take that step, however small, toward meeting your goal today.

Now that you have set up your goals and priorities, plan next week's calendar. Allow a column for each day of the week. Schedule all of your responsibilities and appointments. Add other things from your "to do" list when you find a block of time. Take a red pencil and star every activity that is goal related. What did you find out with this activity? For most of you, the number of red stars will probably be minimal. In addition, your calendar is probably so full there is no room for adding anything new. If one of your goals was to get more exercise, but there is no time for even a half-hour walk, you have a problem. There is no better time than the present to remedy this. Decide which activity is least important and enjoyable for you, and limit your involvement. Try to eliminate one such activity a week for the next month and see if you can unclutter your calendar. If you have difficulty with this, you probably realize that part of your problem stems from your inability to say "no." You cannot protect your priorities unless you learn to decline requests that do not help you achieve your goals. Other people will determine your priorities if you do not protect your own. Is this being selfish? Not at all. It is ensuring that you will develop the talents and qualities that will enable you to give more of yourself to others, rather than give a little of yourself to all needs and requests. Before you agree to a request consider whether it will contribute to your goals or have a high priority for you.

You may agree it all seems very reasonable, but on a day-to-day basis, it may be more difficult. For example, we can assume one of your goals is to do well in your clinical experience. Your bulletin board is scheduled to go up tomorrow. You have traced all of the characters, objects, and letters, and still need to cut them out. The telephone rings. It is the "important other" in your life asking you to go to a movie. What are your choices? You can say "yes" and worry about the bulletin board, or you can say "no" and feel guilty because you are neglecting him or her. The third alternative is to suggest a compromise. Invite him or her to help with the project, and you will furnish the snacks and the T.V. for a rental movie. If the "significant other" in your life is not very agreeable to compromise when one of your major priorities is on the line, it may be time to rethink the relationship!

Another factor in managing your time may be your tendency to be a perfectionist. Remember the admonition "Do it right or don't do it at all," or "good, better, best, never let it rest; til the good is better, and the better best." Do not compromise your standards but look at the alternatives. As a teacher, you will get numerous notes from parents. As a professional you have decided that the only way to respond to a parental note is to type a reply. As a result you spend time after school working on your reply. It would have been much easier to make a phone call, write a response on the bottom of the note, or pen a brief "thank you."

Time management skills are not established overnight. They need to be considered on a continuing basis. These ideas should give you the foundation upon which you can continue to develop and/or improve your time management skills.

There are many books on time management in most libraries. While many of them are written for corporations they all include some ideas you may adapt.

Time Management Books

Collins, K. (1988). Time Management for Teachers. West Nyack, New York: Parker Publishing Company, Inc.

Bliss, E. D. (1976). Getting Things Done, the ABC's of Time Management. New York: Scribners.

Covey, S. (1989). The Seven Habits of Highly Effective People. New York: Simon and Schuster.

chapter twelve
Discipline

As an early clinical student, and later when you become a full-fledged, first-year teacher, you will likely feel great anxiety as you encounter the many facets of running a successful classroom.

Preparedness

Before meeting the children in your class, spend some time acquainting yourself with the community and the school in which you are to teach. Find out the basic philosophies and guidelines set by the school administration, such as behavior and discipline policies, playground rules, cafeteria procedures, scheduling of special subjects, your duties in these areas, and tornado and fire drill safety. Get acquainted with staff members, especially with those at the same grade level with which you are working. Meet the special services personnel who provide needed services for some of your students. Find out what their performance criteria are for the students who qualify for their services, and what is involved in the referral process. Communicate with the school nurse, and go over your class list with him or her so you are aware of any special health needs, such as hearing or vision impairment, asthma concerns, frequent bathroom needs, epilepsy, and diabetes. This will better prepare you to accommodate your students with sensitive understanding. By anticipating a vision or hearing need, for example, you can seat the child appropriately, thus avoiding what might appear to be inattentive or disruptive behavior leading to a discipline concern.

Many schools will have an orientation session for new teachers that is very helpful, but you should make the above contacts on a one-to-one basis to meet the needs of a particular student.

Another aspect of preparedness is to go through all the materials in your room, sorting them to eliminate what is not of immediate use, and organizing the rest to be readily available as you need them. If you have the summer in which to begin preparing, you will want to get teacher manuals of the school's current reading, math, social studies, and science textbooks to peruse and digest over this period of time. And by all means, explore the library and/or learning center to gain firsthand knowledge of what resources are available.

Your first days will be very full as you assimilate all of this information. Then the children arrive.

Continue to make preparedness your mainstay. It will save you many pitfalls. Always have your plans complete and your materials ready in advance of each lesson and project. Children lose interest rapidly if you are cutting art paper or mixing paint as you begin the lesson. When the movie projector or film strip projector is threaded, and plugged in ahead of time, you will rarely lose the students' attention or have significant discipline problems. And when using such materials, be sure you preview them so you can constructively use the film's content to enhance your lesson. When previewing the film, you may discover it is inappropriate for your lesson or for the grade level you are teaching, and you will opt not to use it.

Preparation is also important when reading stories. You should be acquainted with the book before reading it to the children. Knowing your story well will give you a greater sense of confidence, and allow you to make interesting changes in emphasizing certain situations and/or different characters. By knowing the story, you can make use of voice and timing to create anticipation in appropriate places. Children love to be read to and it is an important part of every day. When done well it gives children an enjoyable experience and motivates their interest in learning to read.

Do not be threatened by the child who says, "I've already heard that story." Have a ready response in the positive mode—"Good. I'm glad you've had the fun of reading this story. I'll use you for my helper when we are done." Or, "You will have to come over here by me as my helper and together we will keep the secret about what happens to Little Brown Bear." In other words, accept the information and give the child a sense of approval and importance. And do not interrupt yourself or detract from your reading or the mood by holding the book facing the class or trying to show pictures as you go. Let them know ahead of time that today you want them to make the pictures in their minds as you read, and that the book will be available for them to review for a few days.

Maintaining Order

All of the suggestions for being prepared will help you maintain order. When you are well prepared you have a greater sense of well-being, and the children sense this and flow with you. To maintain order, you must be in control. You need to know, ahead of time, what conditions you need in order to work comfortably in the classroom. If grinding noises such as pencil sharpeners bother you, create an alternate process *before* it becomes a problem. If you do not choose to waste time lining your class up to use the washrooms, but are annoyed by twenty-five individual requests during instructional time, then come up with a plan that works for you. A wooden pass hanging on a peg near the door can be taken by a child needing to use the washroom. When another child sees that it is not in place, he or she will know to wait until it is returned. Kids have the responsibility to take care of their needs, and you have relatively uninterrupted teaching time.

Children need limits. They feel secure in knowing what the rules are and what is expected of them. They want to please, but how can they if they are unaware of what it takes to please? You need to spell out a few helpful rules. The class can contribute their ideas on appropriate rules to make the classroom a pleasant place where everyone can accomplish their work while being considerate of one another.

Even an experienced teacher will be tested when entering a new situation with all new students. The children seem to be asking, by their actions, "How far can we go before you set limits for us?" Once the limits are clearly and firmly established, and consistently carried out, students feel more secure and are free to proceed with the work of the day.

When you need to discipline, convey to the child that you do not approve of the behavior, but that does not mean you do not approve of the child. A good policy is to give praise in an audible way, and to discipline more quietly.

If you have difficulty maintaining order, give attention to how you state things. Do you make positive statements such as, "It is time to clean up," and "Now we are going to the library," or do you ask, "Would you like to see a movie about taking care of your teeth?" The latter demonstrates your insecurity by questioning such matters when you should be in command. You will show the movie; it is part of your lesson. Asking if they would like to see it may bring a few negative responses. Children are quick to sense you are tentative in your control, and such an approach reinforces the idea that you are unsure of yourself. Have the courage to take charge. The children have a whole room full of buddies. They want and need you to be their leader, supporter, and confidant.

Positive Reinforcers

Take a genuine interest in working with the children, exhibiting pleasure and enthusiasm as you teach. This will stimulate the children's attention and responses. They are quick to pick up on your feelings and attitudes. It is not realistic to expect that you can always be cheerful and brimming with energy; but if this is your usual self, children will understand when you have an occasional bad day.

Creating a positive environment may be to take some additional time each day to create a sense of family and community within the group. Children come from different families with great diversity in their abilities to interact and get along with others. They can be guided to see their class as a "family away from home." They work together, play together, eat together, and can benefit from one another through your leadership. Start early to help them assume responsibility for their actions and to keep their classroom and belongings in order. Give positive responses to cooperation, and acknowledge and encourage considerate behavior while helping them be aware that each is a separate, unique individual. They will not always get along with siblings, and will not always get along with each other, but they can be guided to discover thoughtful solutions to their differences.

Children can be very cruel, but can also, with sensitive input, be very supportive. By fostering a supportive classroom climate, you are simultaneously including insecure, often less accepted, children who tend to be discipline problems as they seek attention.

When you are on recess duty and see a couple of the more popular children playing with a lonelier child, be sure to respond and let them know what a special recess that must have been for the usually rejected child. Offer such thought questions as, "How do you think he or she felt about being included? I wonder what it would be like to always be alone?" and perhaps a comment, "Maybe if he or she was included more often by classmates, he or she would learn more about how to play and get along with others. You have been very considerate today and I am really proud of you." These types of observations with your class help to create a good interactive group and good class support.

These types of responses, on your part, are positive reinforcers. Accentuating the positive learning in each situation emits good feelings in you and the children, and encourages them to try again. Use positive statements to give instructions in the "do" mode as opposed to the "don't" mode. Instead of saying, "Don't take too long in the bathroom," try, "You have ten minutes to make use of the bathroom before we board the bus." The first comment suggests you believe they will waste time, while the second comment clearly tells the students that you trust them to do right. Asking a child who is using a crayon to write on the wall, "What is wrong with you?" is less effective than, "Stop writing on the wall!"

Knowing what you want and need in your classroom is only the first step. How you respond to the children's behavior is most important. Positive reinforcement of behavior is preferable to negative consequences for misbehaviors. Here is a list of some of the reinforcers you may want to use.

1. Teacher praise—have a variety of response statements. Need to be personal.

2. Nonverbal approval such as a smile, a pat on the back, a hug.

3. Recognition—"Sarah is sitting quietly."

4. Privilege—being line leader or messenger.

5. Earn time to work on a special project.

6. Class party for something done especially well by the class.

7. Special movie.

8. Free time for game activities (other than educational games).

9. Time alone with the teacher.

10. Lunch with the teacher.

11. Taking a special item or a classroom pet home overnight or for the weekend.

12. A happy-gram to the parents.

13. A call home to the parents by the child or the teacher to relate a good experience.

14. Earn extra points or stars on a chart for certain activities (Caution: This can be very defeative to the child who seemingly never earns a star and looks at the many stars earned by others).

15. Special classroom award—these must be numerous and of a great variety (both academic and non-academic) so that a majority may win one.

Unfortunately, too many times teachers accept proper behavior as the norm and fail to acknowledge and reinforce it by making a comment, "It makes me feel so good to see all of you working so well." Reinforcement may often keep disruptive behavior from occurring. Reinforcement must be sincere, not over-done, and given as appropriate.

Having a plan to prevent behavior problems from developing is a great start. You also need to have a plan for dealing with discipline problems when they occur.

Consequences

As part of your preparedness, it is wise to develop ideas, philosophies, and expectations on how you might handle discipline. Know what type of classroom environment you are comfortable with, and try to be aware of what behaviors you can realistically expect from the students. Next, consider some possible conse-quences to use when the desired behaviors do not occur. Realize that in your clinical and student teaching experiences you will need to align yourself with the procedures used by your cooperating teacher, and to make use of additional techniques as appropriate. Keep developing and expanding your philosophies and ideas. Refer to Chapter Thirteen (Evaluation). Are there items in any of the following five listed categories that could be altered to improve the students' behavior?

Developing ideas and deciding on the consequences you will use for misbehavior is an individual matter. Whenever possible, the consequence should be one that works for that particular student, is quickly administered, does not single the student out for humiliation and ridicule, is one you are comfortable with, and fits the crime.

Possible consequences include:

1. Time out in your classroom, another classroom, or the office (avoid the hall; children have been known to leave the building and outsiders do come in).

If the student is being inattentive or disturbing others, a time-out space within the room is useful, and allows the student to give more attention to the task. Some classrooms provide a couple of carrels or "offices" (can be made from refrigerator boxes—painted and decorated by the students most in need of an occasional quiet area) where students can work without feeling they have been punished. It allows you to separate disruptive children for a while without humiliating them in front of their peers.

There are times when you will want to remove the child from the classroom for a brief time and place him or her in another classroom (previously agreed to by the other teacher). You must be sensitive not to add to their problems by sending them to a grade level that will somehow humiliate them. Shaming, humiliating, or ridiculing a student is destructive. The children who will cause you the greatest difficulty have already been hurt in many ways, and are very needy for attention and peer acceptance. You must develop positive, reinforcing strategies to deliver necessary discipline.

Time in the office is another way to give the child a quiet place with adult supervision away from the distractions of the entire class. Be well acquainted with your principal's philosophies on discipline to ensure the child will not be laboriously writing, "I will not talk in class" one hundred times.

2. Loss of free time, stay in for recess, stay after school.

Use free time as an effective discipline technique. Recess is a less likely alternative because you cannot leave children unattended in the room while you take a brief break. Also, there are children who do not like recess because of the weather or because they are stressed by their feeling of not belonging. These children will do anything to avoid recess—even neglect getting work done or misbehave if they learn they can remain inside.

It will take time to arrive at the best consequence for a particular child. If the non-desired behavior continues and you have not found the most effective consequence for that individual, try another approach.

Keeping children after school in any situation requires that you first contact the parents. If this delays the detention to another day, the discipline immediately becomes less effective. Students will forget why they are being disciplined. However, if a child is bused and the parent is inconvenienced by the detention, this can be an effective punishment. With the parent's cooperation and inconvenience, the child hears about it both at school and at home.

3. Loss of a privilege.

This can be effective as long as the privilege is significantly important to that child.

4. Reprimand—spoken only to that student.

If the misbehavior is one covered on the classroom chart of rules for the class, it could be pointed out to the child. It is also a good time to quietly communicate with the child to see if you can better understand the child's present distraction. Is he or she frustrated with the lesson? Was he or she annoyed by another child and now feels misunderstood by you? You need to take time to listen and understand. Try not to jump to conclusions or operate from your own perceptions of the situation, thus making the child a victim. The child may be wrong, but value him or her enough to listen. Then help the child learn from the experience.

5. A call or a note to parents.

Communication with parents is important, and should occur as needed and appropriate. Ongoing contact is far more effective than no contact, but it should not be overused. Like giving positive input to children, you should also call the parents when their child has had some better days following problematic ones. You should be knowledgeable of the family situation before calling. If both parents work, call in the evening or at work if the parents have given you the number. Sometimes, children will discipline themselves a bit better knowing you are willing to call their parents. With one highly disruptive and destructive youngster whose father worked nights, the teacher elected to disturb the father's sleep. Naturally the father was not pleased, so it did have a real impact on the young boy's future behavior. Whereas one does not like to have a child set up to fear his father's wrath, some situations dictate more drastic action if it will benefit the other children who also have need of you.

These five consequences are the most frequently used. No consequence should be used for every child even in similar situations. Some children have been yelled at so much in the home, they are seemingly immune to a loud or raised voice, while highly sensitive children respond to a severe look.

Knowing the Children

It takes time, but getting to know each child is an important part of the first few weeks of school. And as each student grows and changes, you will continue to learn more throughout the year. Children need to feel wanted and liked by you, so it is essential you give them a warm accepting welcome each day, listen well to the various little items they wish to relate to you, and be sensitive to those who show special needs. This type of awareness is used in carrying out case studies (Chapter Four). Though you will not always be carrying out formal case studies on every child, you will be developing this type of mental file on each individual in your care.

What do you do about the child to whom you cannot easily relate? Naturally, you will be more attracted to some children. This is not usually a problem as you will maintain a fair and friendly demeanor and operate by your philosophies for helping children develop and learn. But when there are children you have difficulty liking, you will need to consciously reach out to them while helping yourself determine what causes this feeling in you. One teacher had five girls who fit this category. They hung on her, pestered and crowded her, until she feared she would lose her composure with them. Several weeks later she awoke one night from a dream and realized that she acted the same way as a third-grader.

They needed her and her attention as she had once needed the approval of her teacher so long ago. Once she realized this, the girls no longer seemed so annoying. She was able to give them genuine attention and they subsequently became less demanding. Many times some of our own early needs are mirrored back to us through the children we teach.

Then there is the matter of chemistry between people. Sometimes, the chemistry between two people is not there or is counter-productive. If after three to four weeks of school the situation does not improve, discuss it with the appropriate teacher to see if the child could be moved to another classroom. If not, you need to do all you can in making positive adjustments in your own behavior so the child will not be the loser. Also, seek help from the social worker. You may choose to speak to him or her before talking it over with any other teacher.

The following are examples of problems that actually do occur. Think each one through. What kinds of additional information would you consider important to pursue in each case? What help should be given? What form of discipline might be appropriate? Whose help might you seek for further clarification and support?

After studying each case, continue to read on to find the solutions to these problems as they actually occurred.

In summary, know what you want and need to make your classroom a happy environment for you and the children. Know how to fulfill your wants and needs, and what to do if your initial plans do not work. Remember that there is always a solution to the problem—though some solutions may take longer than others.

Classroom Problems

1. You and another teacher team teach for certain activities. You teach her music class, while she teaches physical education (P.E.) It is the week before Christmas and the principal has arranged for Santa to visit that day. Your teammate returns from P.E. with the news that Robbie (who seldom cooperates) misbehaved and cannot attend Santa's visit. Robbie comes from an underprivileged environment and would really be upset by being excluded. You question the fairness of the punishment, but have always respected your team teacher's decisions. What do you do?

2. John is a recent student in your room. His records have not yet arrived. He is obviously a disturbed child. He disrupts the room constantly, and interferes with other children by scribbling on their papers and taking their belongings. Other teachers report poor behavior on the playground. His mother seems aware of all these things but shrugs her shoulders when they are brought to her attention. How should you handle this?

3. Lisa is in your first-grade class. She did not talk during kindergarten. School personnel, feeling that she was of average intelligence, promoted her to first grade. How will you decide what to do when assigning her to a reading group?

4. Your school has several children who are Jehovah's Witnesses. This is your first experience with having one in your room. The booklet (presented to you by the parents) outlines what is expected of the student and of you as the teacher. Timmy is not to participate in the pledge to the flag, holiday art, classroom celebrations of the holidays, or birthday celebrations. Timmy is a very quiet, withdrawn child who seems to accept all these things. Because of an injury to his foot, he has remained behind during P.E. period. He whispers to you that it is his birthday. You always present a pencil to each student on his or her birthday. How will you handle this?

5. Wes is the class clown. He enjoys being the center of attention in his sixth-grade class. During work time he makes loud animal noises, tells jokes, and draws provocative pictures he holds up for the class to see. How could you change this behavior?

6. Madeline is a third-grade student who is extrememely disruptive. While the classroom rule states that students must raise their hands and be recognized, Madeline continues to make remarks such as, "I don't like dumb social studies." You decide to punish her by subtracting minutes from recess. After three interruptions in which she lost five minutes, she has no recess period left. When you remind Madeline of this, she remarks, "I don't care if I never go to recess, I don't like boring social studies." How will you handle this?

7. Tom is a third-grade student. He is very quiet, never disruptive, seldom responds in class, and has yet to finish an assignment. The social worker has informed you that his home situation is very poor. The family lives on a disability check. The father is seldom sober. Although you have not had a conference with her, you have been told that Tom's mother, when informed that her son does not complete his work, says, "So what?" What do you propose to do?

Outcomes to Classroom Problems as They Occurred

The following outcomes of the classroom problems are presented for your information. You may agree or disagree with the outcomes. The important thing to remember is that you must consider these types of problems when forming your own classroom management theories. You may read, observe, and adapt ideas from other sources, but in the end, you must decide how to solve the problems in your classroom.

1. This problem really has two components: dealing with Robbie's behavior and your relationship with the team teacher. In this particular example, Robbie's teacher felt the punishment to be too extreme. She discussed an alternative punishment with the team teacher. They agreed that staying in for recess would be an acceptable alternative. She informed Robbie of the change. It is interesting to note that while not excluded from visiting Santa, Robbie refused to participate when the time came.

2. It is not unusual, as in the case of John, for a student's records to be delayed. In this case, the teacher asked for outside help. The social worker was called upon to observe John in the classroom. He was referred for vision and hearing testing by the nurse, and the principal was asked to pursue the missing records. John was referred to the Pupil Personnel Committee when the records finally arrived. The records indicated his placement should have been in a special education classroom. The mother, obviously feeling stigmatized by this placement, stated that he was a first-grader and he was placed in a first-grade class. After placement in the appropriate special education class, with mainstreaming to the regular class for certain activities, John's behavior changed dramatically. He was able to function at his academic level and a great deal of his frustration was resolved.

3. In this case, you may also feel there are some unanswered questions. The teacher placed Lisa in the average reading group, while seeking some answers. The kindergarten teacher confirmed that she had never heard Lisa speak, the nurse's records revealed normal vision and hearing, paper and pencil tasks indicated normal intelligence, and a conference with the mother (father did not attend) revealed that Lisa spoke at home. Lisa was meeting weekly with the school speech therapist, in the hopes that in a one-on-one situation she might speak. To date this had not happened. During the reading group, the teacher called on Lisa daily until, one day, she started to read. It turned out she had a severe speech impediment. Following the lesson, the teacher sent Lisa on an errand to the office. She then proceeded to discuss the problem with the class, explaining how important it was that Lisa not be teased about her speech. It was amazing how Lisa blossomed after that. With the help of supportive classmates and an understanding teacher, Lisa became quite gregarious. It is possible that at the start of her school experience, she began to talk and someone made fun of her, so she resolved not to speak aloud again.

4. This is a very common situation in many schools. On this particular occasion, Timmy finished all of his daily work, which was a first for him. The teacher awarded him the pencil for having completed all of his work. How you would handle the situation in your particular classroom would depend on what decision you, as a teacher, can live with. Some teachers have no problem following the "letter of the law" as it were, while others would find it more difficult. If you have reservations about this type of restriction, it would be a good thing to discuss it with the parents, *before* a problem arises.

5. Wes was obviously in need of attention from the teacher and his peers. This was not a situation that the teacher believed would be solved quickly. When Wes was engaging in disruptive behavior, the teacher arranged for him to have time out in another class. She also created opportunities for Wes to spend time with her during the noon hour. This not only served to give him the attention he sought, but was also instrumental in helping the teacher understand his behavior. In addition, she and Wes explored ways he might channel his disruptive behavior into more acceptable bids for attention. In

this case, working with the kindergarten class, helping with art, and reading stories provided an outlet for Wes that was very beneficial.

6. In Madeline's case, the teacher could have tried several approaches. She decided that the loss of recess was not working. She elected to try time out in the classroom for each time Madeline spoke out. Many times, consequences have to be adapted to each student. As in this case, many students are not especially upset by losing the recess privilege, especially in cold and inclement weather.

7. There are many "Toms" in the schools today. Unfortunately, this situation remained unresolved when Tom was observed two years later in his fifth-grade classroom. As a future teacher, what are some of the things you need to understand in this situation? What will help you clarify the problem? Refer to Maslow's hierachy of needs, from lowest to highest. It includes physiological needs (food, water, shelter), safety needs (sense of secure job or income), social needs (acceptance by others, affection), and esteem needs (desire for recognition). Where in this hierarchy is Tom's mother? Wondering if she is going to have money to put groceries on the table this week puts her at the very bottom. Do you wonder that her comment was, "So what?" when told about Tom's inability to finish his work? She has more important things to worry about. As a teacher, you may have to accept that you may not get assistance from the parents. In addition, you may have to become the social agent to provide assistance. In many communities, you, as the child's teacher, become the only contact the families have, and as such, you must make the attempt to connect them with the proper agency. Difficult as it may be for teachers to accept, children like Tom may be beyond the scope of the classroom teacher's help. Should this keep you from trying? Not at all. Give the problem all the resources you have available and remember your day-to-day support may mean a great deal in the years to come.

chapter thirteen
Evaluation

Evaluation is an ongoing and often many-faceted process. As the student, you will be evaluated in certain areas by both your university supervisor and your cooperating teacher. You will also be involved in the process as you critique your own participation in the classroom. In addition, how you present yourself while in the school will be noticed by your principal, which in many cases has paid off for students when they seek a teaching job. And never underestimate the ability of children to do their own style of evaluation.

Evaluation should be used as a constructive process, identifying where you are, and taking steps toward improvement and growth. Make note of the positive aspects of your performance, as well as the things that need improvement. Each time you work with a group of children, whether it be walking them through the hall to gym, correcting behavior, or teaching a lesson, ask yourself how you feel about the way you handled a situation. What went well, what might have gone better, and what can you try the next time. Talk it over with your university supervisor and/or cooperating teacher to gain additional constructive input. Though you will be able to sense what you believe went well, and what could go better, you will not always be able to identify *why* it went well or how to improve on it. That is why your support people are available to help you.

You are used to being evaluated in a formal manner by tests and grades, but this is different. You will not stand up the first time, teach a perfect lesson, and receive an A+. Instead, you will engage in many aspects of the classroom, sometimes working one-to-one, listening to a small group read, helping a few children practice a specific skill like addition facts, assisting on recess duty, or reading to the class. Always try to be sensitive to what you believe went really well, or what may have frustrated you, and then seek input. This is all part of an ongoing process of self-evaluation.

Before reading a story to the class, ask your cooperating teacher to give you feedback. This will aide you in developing your skills as well as learning new techniques for working with the group. The more input you receive and use constructively, the more you grow toward becoming a successful teacher. You learn and mature as you participate and receive supportive feedback.

Another dimension of evaluation is to assess the school and classroom to which you are assigned. There is an outline provided to help you focus attention on five specific aspects: the classroom, classroom management, the students, lesson delivery, and student/teacher interaction. You will observe strengths and weaknesses, pick up ideas you may incorporate into your teaching style, and raise questions to be answered later.

The outline referred to here is found on pages 94-97 and may be altered to suit your situation. Though some items may be too complex for you at this juncture, they can help you become aware of some important dimensions within the classroom.

Realize that all classes are different; all teachers are different in ability, temperament, and personality; and not all teachers are model teachers. On occasion, you may learn by seeing what *not* to do. If you use this outline, taking notes as you go, it could help you share with your instructor at the close of this clinical experience. There are occasions, though not frequent, when the personality of two individuals (cooperating teacher and early clinical student) makes it difficult for you to have a meaningful clinical experience. You must make an effort, but must also communicate immediately with your university supervisor. He or she will assess the situation, make suggestions for improvement, or move you to another classroom if the situation is beyond remediation.

Remember, throughout this process you must maintain your professionalism and tact. With your limited exposure, you cannot expect to be an authority in any of these areas. Therefore, observe, review the outline, make appropriate notes, raise questions for consideration, and participate in discussions with your university supervisor and college classmates back on campus.

While you are working on your clinical experience, your university supervisor will visit and make some on-site observations of your participation. This is usually a good time to express any concerns you might have, such as not being allowed to share in the children's learning activities, or feeling you are used solely as a paper grader and ditto-machine operator. He or she can give you suggestions to solve the problem and, if desirable, can communicate your concerns to the teacher.

It will be your responsibility to keep your university supervisor informed about when you are in charge of a classroom activity. He or she would prefer to see you present your lesson. If logistics do not allow this, at least let him or her see you in another situation, such as reading a story to the group. Being observed will very likely make you nervous, but try your best to see it as an opportunity for growth. If such things as voice projection, speaking speed, interesting inflection of voice when reading, or showing more enthusiasm can be brought to your attention, then it can only help you to improve the next time. He or she will also give you feedback on what you did well, such as involving the entire group in a discussion or keeping the children's attention. In the event your university supervisor cannot fit your presentation into his or her schedule, be sure to ask your cooperating teacher to critique your lesson or activity. It is beneficial to have both sources of input to bring out different ideas. If you do not receive this feedback, giving you reinforcement for what went well and suggestions for growth, you are the loser. It is not simply a matter of right or wrong; it is taking time to review what you set out to accomplish, how well you succeeded, and what you might do differently to better attain your goals.

At this first clinical level, your university supervisor and cooperating teacher will help you, but will not condemn you for making errors unless you show no evidence of effort. They will watch for the following, fully aware this is your first clinical experience. Their feedback should include supportive and constructive comments.

1. Appearance: as a professional adult.
2. Voice: pitch level, volume, projection.
3. Speech: too fast or slow, correct usage (grammar and pronunciation).
4. Mobility: Are you cemented to one location or are you comfortable moving among the group, giving all the children a sense of your nearness?
5. Posture: Your positioning of yourself, especially when writing on the board with your back to the children. Also, when seated, do you have bad posture?
6. Awareness of students: Demonstrate progress in knowing their names, attempt to include all children (even those who do not raise their hands). Give adequate time for responses and give encouragement to less outgoing youngsters. Give praise appropriately.
7. Enthusiasm: Are you able to project a real interest in what you are doing, thus maintaining attention from the group?
8. Lesson: too long, too short, too much content, or not enough. Were the components of the lesson plan evident? (Anticipatory set, statement of objectives, input, modeling, checking for understanding, independent activity, and evaluation or closure).
9. Discipline: Were you aware of every child? Did you have everyone's attention before starting? Did you call on an inattentive child to help bring his or her attention back to the lesson? If you made a threat such as, "If you throw your pencil again, you will return to your seat," did you carry it out? If you said, "I will only call on those who are quiet and raise their hands," did you follow through?

Notes taken while you are being observed are strictly for giving you thorough feedback. They are not filed anywhere without your knowledge. They are only used if necessary to file a deficiency report on your first clinical experience. Though this format is not universal, some form of evaluation is beneficial in providing students with supportive direction toward eliminating weaknesses and achieving individual goals.

A teacher education deficiency report is filled out and filed by the university supervisor if he or she believes your performance or behavior raises concern about your suitability for the teaching profession due to deficiencies in academic performance, professional skills, or attitude. There is room for a brief statement about the deficiency with any recommendations for remediation, when appropriate. It is signed by the university supervisor and the early clinical student, with copies going to the appropriate areas within the elementary education department.

This could be a formal identification, for the records, that an early clinical student with a serious speech or grammar problem had difficulty with the clinical experience. It would recommend the individual receive remedial assistance before being encouraged to proceed in the education field.

Sometimes a deficiency report is filed when the early clinical student fails. This provides written evidence of the student's clinical experience, and is reviewed and signed by the student.

The formal evaluation report of your first clinical experience is filled out by you and, in part, by your cooperating teacher. It goes into your file in the student teaching office for future reference, if necessary, but is not a part of your final senior student teacher evaluation in your permanent file.

About two-thirds of the one-page form is filled out by you and includes a definition of your clinical setting (city, school, grade level, subject); a description of the students with whom you worked (including racial, ethnic, social, economic, and special education mix); and a description of the work you did in your clinical experience. The bottom portion is completed by your cooperating teacher. He or she is asked to rate your performance, based on the objectives of this particular experience, by checking excellent, very good, average, or poor, and making any additional comments in the five lines provided. Then it is signed by you, your university supervisor and your cooperating teacher.

Student Teacher Observation Guide

Focus Area 1—The Classroom	Comments
1. Does the physical space appear to be pleasing and useful to the student? (arrangement of desks, area designated for different activities, decorations)	
2. Do the following appear to be appropriate for the age of the students? a. classroom materials? b. equipment?	
3. Is the classroom easily accessible to: a. regular education classrooms? b. rest rooms? c. lunchrooms, playground, gym, music, and art?	
4. Is the room located in a quiet or noisy part of the building?	
5. Is the classroom too hot or too cold?	

6. What is on the bulletin boards:
    a. student work?
    b. charts of student progress?
    c. learning materials?

7. Are classroom rules posted?

8. Are consequences for breaking the rules posted?

9. Are fire and tornado routes posted?

Focus Area 2—Classroom Management	**Comments**

1. How does the teacher handle daily routines:
    a. taking roll?
    b. lunch count?
    c. hall passes?
    d. checking out and returning materials?
    e. assignments for absentees?

2. How does the teacher organize teaching materials?

3. Where do students place completed papers?

4. How are papers returned?

5. Where are additional supplies for students (paper, pencils, paste)?

6. How does the teacher deal with notes to go home?

7. What responsibilities for daily routines are delegated to students?

8. What provisions are made for a substitute:
    a. name tags?
    b. seating chart?
    c. supplemental lesson plans?

9. How does the teacher communicate with parents:
    a. readers home?

	Comments
b. flash cards home? c. weekly work home? d. progress report? e. homework assignments? f. newsletter?	

Focus Area 3—The Students	**Comments**

1. What is the general makeup of this class:
  a. number of students?
  b. race?
  c. ability?
  d. ratio of boys to girls?
  e. special problems?	

2. Are there any mainstreamed children?	
3. If so, are instructional activities modified for this child?	

4. Do some students leave the room for special help:
  a. resource room?
  b. Chapter I reading or math?
  c. physical therapy?
  d. speech therapy?
  e. social worker?	

5. Are there any children repeating this grade?	

Focus Area 4—The Lesson Delivery	**Comments**

1. How did the teacher begin the lesson:
  a. motivating techniques?
  b. review of previous lesson?
  c. objectives clearly stated?	

2. How did the teacher distribute and collect materials?	

3. How did the teacher give directions:
  a. spoken in clear voice?
  b. students were made to understand what was expected of them?	

	Comments
4. Was the handwriting on the board and the written material easy to read?	
5. Was variety reflected in the types of questioning?	
6. How was the lesson closed?	
7. What method of evaluation was used?	
8. What provisions were made for students who finished the assignment early?	

Focus Area 5—Teacher-Student Interactions	**Comments**
1. How did the teacher relate the materials and the method to varying levels of ability?	
2. Did the teacher show respect for student ideas?	
3. Did the teacher praise the class for good performance?	
4. How did the teacher draw out the reticent child and help the over-exuberant child be part of the group?	

5. What other types of teacher interaction occurred?
   a. warm?
   b. critical?
   c. energetic?
   d. neutral?
   e. directive?
   f. non-directive?
   g. supportive?	

chapter fourteen
Cultural Shock and the Three Rs

If you have traveled to another country, even one where they speak the same language, you have experienced cultural shock. Things are done differently. Words for objects may mean one thing to you, something quite different to them. In many countries, teaching materials are not as abundant and the technology is not as advanced as they are at home.

Early clinical students entering the elementary school classroom from the university campus sometimes experience cultural shock. The transition from the campus, where much of the emphasis is on research and new methods, to the public school, where children are being educated, sometimes seems as far removed as traveling from one country to another.

As you enter your clinical experience, you may question why much of the educational research remains theoretical with little classroom impact, or why it is implemented years later yet heralded as the new approach to teaching. To fully understand why methods lag far behind research data, you need to understand how a classroom teacher is exposed to new methods. The most common ways are by reading professional journals, attending meetings or inservice workshops, and talking with colleagues. Unfortunately, in many schools the day-to-day working life of the classroom teacher offers little time for such interaction. In addition, innovations for teaching math or reading require additional funds for supplies. Many school districts do not have the money to implement the programs even when the staff recommends a change. Your cultural shock will be lessened greatly if you keep these ideas in mind as you make the transition to the classroom.

Presented in this chapter are some of the methods being implemented in today's schools. They may be present in the classroom where you have your clinical experience. If they are, ask yourself: "Does this really work?" "If not, why not?" "Are there ways I could use some of the ideas, but not the total concept?" "Could it work with some of the students, but not with others?" "How does this method of teaching tie in with what I have learned about the theories of Piaget or Bruner?"

Several new approaches to teaching math are used in the elementary schools. One of these, "Touch Math," is a method of teaching addition, subtraction, multiplication, and division to students. It involves having the students tap reference points on numerals to count out sums, differences, and products.*

1 2 3 4 5 6 7 8 9

To add two numbers, the children touch each reference point in the proper sequence and count at each touch. The progression is as follows: (1) children draw dots on each number as an addition problem and count the dots, (2) they draw smaller dots and count as they draw them, (3) they count from one of the addends (3 and 4) and count the dots on the second, saying 3, 4-5-6-7, (4) they touch the number without the dots to arrive at the sum. The idea is that having repeated the procedure enough times, students will have memorized the addition facts. To subtract with this method, students touch the larger number, say its name, tap each point on the smaller number and count backward, 9 minus 4, says 9, touches 4 and counts 8-7-6-5. Multiplication and division are taught using skip counting. For example, to calculate 5 times 3 or 3 times 5, students count by 3s and touch a dot position on the 5 for each multiple.

Teachers prefer the method because it is easy and students are successful. Even the slowest student is able to come up with correct answers.

You will be able to see some of the problems with this process. While observing the method in the classroom, you may want to formulate some additional questions: "Do the students understand what they are doing?" "Will all students make the transition to having the facts in memory or will it continue to be a process on which they will rely in the upper grades?" "Would it work for Joe, but not for Mary?" "Is the classroom teacher using it as a supplement or as a total program?"

"Mathematics Their Way" is another program being adopted by many schools. The idea behind the program is to develop an understanding of math through concrete materials. The program recommends using a variety of familiar materials to provide motivation for learning, exploration, and problem-solving. Many of the activities are ongoing.

One example is the calendar activity. The teacher has number cards on the chalkboard, identified as yesterday, today, and tomorrow. The student comes up and responds to the teacher's questions. "What is today?" (sixth) "What was yesterday?" (fifth) "What will tomorrow be?" (seventh). The teacher then pops the balloon under yesterday's card, and blows one up for today. The teacher then asks the students, "How many days have we been in school?" The student adds a number to the adding tape on the chalkboard. Additional activities may include: measuring today's temperature on the thermometer; measuring to see how much the plant has grown; or checking students' weight and height on a monthly basis.

---

* Flexer, Roberta, and Naomi Rosenberger. "Beware of Tapping Pencils." Arithmetic Teacher, 34 (January 1987): 6-10

The program emphasizes the students' ability to use math to interpret the world around them.

Programs in Reading

The elementary schools are using the "Whole Language" approach to reading. This is a holistic teaching approach that is gaining popularity in a number of schools. Its success is due, in part, to its approach to learning. Children learn from general to specific, from familiar to unfamiliar. How children learn is linked to what children want to know. Instead of using basal readers or prepackaged programs, teachers use a variety of literature. Big books, library books, poems, magazine articles, comic strips, and advertisements are all used to help children discuss how language is used.

Teachers and children work together to plan a theme to serve as the core for the learning activities. If the theme is bears, the teacher would begin by asking, "What do you know about bears?" The ideas are recorded as students respond. The list serves as a word bank for later activities. Daily activities built around the theme could include: recording ideas; shared reading; silent reading; singing and dramatic reading; and writing to communicate what they have learned.

Teachers are very enthusiastic about the program. It requires teacher training, teacher-developed materials, and parental education.

Some of the methods may be used in schools to which you are assigned for your clinical experience. The opportunity to observe these and other programs provides a real opportunity for learning. There are certain ideas you should keep in mind.

First, be open-minded rather than critical. If you believe the teacher or the school district is behind in implementing curriculum change, ask yourself if it is due to a of lack of funds, or if the teacher is about to retire and does not want to try something new. It also could be they already tried it and decided it did not work.

Second, when observing a new program (many programs are simply old ideas wearing a new label), ask yourself questions about how well it seems to meet the needs of the students. Sit down with individual students and ask them how they arrived at a particular answer, if they like this way of counting, or if they understand what they are doing.

Third, observe more than one classroom using the method and how another teacher handles the same idea. Ask yourself if it works better in one classroom than another, or if it is the students or the teacher who make the difference. Determine if one teacher has adapted the idea as a supplement to his or her regular program and if it improves its effectiveness.

Fourth, check to see what the force is behind the program's implementation. Was it the result of a decision involving the entire staff? Was it recommended by a few teachers who attended a workshop and in their enthusiasm decided it should involve the total staff? Was it recommended by a committee? Did the idea come from the administration with little teacher input? The successful implementation of any new program is dependent on total staff involvement and cooperation. Without this, even the best program will suffer from lack of support.

With these ideas in mind, you should be able to effectively evaluate the programs you observe. Children are individuals, and have different learning styles. Sometimes teachers use one ideology and forget there is no single method by which children learn. Try to be objective and learn as much as you can. It will serve you well when you step into your own classroom.

Penmanship—D'Nealian

Despite technological advances, handwriting is still a most essential skill. People, regardless of their profession, have to write, sign, or compute something almost every day.

If you look around, you will see many examples of poor, unattractive, and illegible handwriting. There is no single, easy answer to poor handwriting, but, as would-be teachers, you need to be aware of ways to help improve penmanship.

Typically, children first learn to print their names, letters of the alphabet, and numbers. This requires hand-eye coordination and small-muscle control. Often, children are taught to print using capital letters. They must be retaught that capitals are for the beginning letters of their names, followed by lowercase letters. This can be discouraging for them.

Learning to write is a developmental process and requires readiness of hand-eye coordination and small-muscle control on the part of the individual child. As in all types of learning activities, children will progress at different rates.

For years, children have been taught to form letters by making circles and straight lines (sometimes referred to as balls and sticks). This means learning to put the necessary circles and straight lines together to create the picture, or letter. Often, this requires making two to four separate and correctly placed strokes of the pencil.

If a child lacks coordination and/or small-muscle development, has to unlearn letter formations, and cannot see a real likeness to the writing, he or she can become discouraged from the outset.

In the 1970s, Scott Foresman came out with the D'Nealian handwriting program, which has been used in a number of elementary schools. You should become acquainted with this program since you will likely encounter it in your school experiences.

In D'Nealian, the forms of most lowercase letters are the basic forms of the corresponding cursive letters. The letters are each made with one continuous stroke except for dotting the letters i and j and crossing the letters f, t, and x. Because most of the letters are made with a continuous stroke, there is less frustration for the beginner and an earlier sense of success.

The transition from lowercase to cursive is very easy and comes naturally to many children, except for f, r, s, v, and z. D'Nealian letters become cursive letters with the addition of joining strokes. And because of the similarities in appearance, it is easy for students to read D'Nealian cursive, while the transition from circles and sticks to cursive is difficult reading for many.

D'Nealian Manuscript Alphabet

D'Nealian Cursive Alphabet

D'Nealian Numbers

chapter fifteen
Children's Literature

One of your first opportunities to participate in the classroom may be to read a story to the children. Hopefully, it will be a story you have prepared ahead of time. Since some cooperating teachers may request you do it without much advance notice, it is always a good idea to have a familiar book in mind.

Certain universities now require a course in children's literature for those majoring in elementary education. If it is not a requirement at your university, make it one of your electives.

In addition, you need to spend time exploring the university, town, and school libraries, and getting to know the librarian.

A knowledge of what is available in children's literature will help you choose a daily story to read aloud, and will assist you in recommending books to students and parents.

Books have a further use in the classroom, and that is to teach values. Reading a book may be a subtle way to achieve a change in attitude that would take much longer by any direct teaching method.

One teacher had the following experience while finishing out the year for a colleague. The class was a fourth-grade class in a rural area. The classroom presented a unique situation. The students were always in trouble when outside the classroom. Part of this was due to their lack of sensitivity to other people's feelings. This, combined with a lack of respect for adults, often led to trouble on the playground and in the cafeteria. They spent their leisure time shooting birds with B B guns out of trees, throwing stones at anything that moved, and destroying property. They were known to everyone as the "terrors of the community."

The teacher tried a variety of approaches to the problem and seemed to get nowhere. Since they really enjoyed the daily story hour, the teacher decided to see if an appropriate book could be located. The local librarian recommended *Along Came a Dog,* by Meindert DeJong (1958). The story is about a stray dog who becomes the protector of a little red hen. The hen differs from the rest of the flock not only in color but because she has no feet. This makes her an outsider, vulnerable to attack by the rest of the flock. The dog's job as protector is further complicated by the hired man, who takes the dog away from the farm whenever he sees him.

"In timid misery the big dog crawled up to the seat, flowed up to the seat as if there wasn't a bone in his body. The man slammed the door shut and started the car... The dog lifted his hopeless eyes to the little red hen."

"He was back. Twice he's been taken away, twice now he'd come back. And if the man were to take him away thirty times, he'd come back thirty times. He wasn't dim-witted, he knew he wasn't wanted here. But everytime he was taken away, he's come back. It wasn't a plan in the big dog's mind. It was a need, a desperation to have a home. He was going to have a home! It was that simple... The little red hen was his to guard and protect, and he was going to be the man's and this was going to be his home."*

The book was not discussed, simply read a chapter or two a day. Occasionally, the teacher would glance up from reading and notice tears in the students' eyes. Slowly, the students' behavior outside the classroom changed. There were fewer reports of fights on the playground or expulsions from the cafeteria. The principal and staff members commented on their new attitudes. Individual students demonstrated more compassion. One student brought in an injured bird to be nursed back to life. Another boy, whose family was giving him a dog for his birthday, insisted on going to the local animal shelter to pick out the dog. He named him Stray Dog. A definite shift in attitude had taken place. One author writing with a great deal of sensitivity had been able to reach these students in a short time, and transformed their behavior. A change like this might have taken months or even years by any other method, if it had happened at all.

The study of high-quality literature should be a vital part of every elementary school teacher's program. Familiarize yourself with the available books and work closely with the school librarians for assistance. Teachers can use examples from literature to nurture qualities of character and behavior. History and biographies can provide role models that will broaden students' horizons. Stories can reinforce enduring standards of conduct and enhance moral awareness and self-recognition. *The Little Engine that Could* teaches young children perseverance; Scrooge illustrates the ability to change from bad to good; *Captain Courageous* portrays a spoiled boy's transformation into a loyal friend; and *The Adventures of Huckleberry Finn* details a young boy's struggle with his conscience as he rejects the norms of behavior to defend his friend Jim. Good literature for children is an essential tool for the classroom teacher. Learn all you can, ask for advice from other teachers and librarians, and explore all the possibilities of literature in your classroom.

The Newbery Medal

The Newbery Medal is awarded annually by the Children's Service Division of the American Library Association. It was first offered in 1921 by

---

* *Dejong, Meindert. Along Came A Dog. Harper, 1958.*

Frederic C. Milcher (1879-1963) of the R.R. Bowker Company as an incentive for better quality in children's books. Named after John Newbery, the famous 18th century publisher of children's books, it is given annually to the author of the most distinguished contribution to American literature for children published during the preceding year.

Newbery Award Books

*denotes Newbery Honor Book

Year	Author	Title
1922	Van Loon	*The Story of Mankind*
	Colum	* *Golden Fleece and the Heroes Who Lived Before Achilles*
	Hawes	* *The Great Quest*
	Marshall	* *Cedric The Forester*
	Bowen	* *The Old Tobacco Shop*
	Meigs	* *Windy Hill*
1923	Lofting	*The Voyages of Doctor Dolittle*
1924	Hawes	*The Dark Frigate*
1925	Finger	*Tales From Silver Lands*
	Moore	* *Nicholas*
	Parrish	* *Dream Coach*
1926	Chrisman	*Shen of the Sea*
	Colum	* *Voyagers*
1927	James	*Smoky, The Cowhorse*
1928	Mukerji	*Gay Neck, The Story of a Pigeon*
	Young	* *The Wonder Smith and His Son*
	Snedeker	* *Downright Dencey*
1929	Kelly	*The Trumpeter of Krakow*
	Gag	* *Millions of Cats*
	Bennett	* *Pigtail of Ah Lee Ben Loo*
	Hallock	* *The Boy Who Was*
	Meigs	* *Clearing Weather*
	Moon	* *Runaway Papoose*
	Whitney	* *Tod of the Fens*
1930	Field	*Hitty, Her First Hundred Years*
	Eaton	* *Daughter of the Seine*
	Miller	* *Pran of Albania*
	Hurd	* *Jumping-Off Place*
	Young	* *The Tangle-Coated Horse and Other Tales*

Year	Author	Title
	Adams	* *Vaino*
	Swift	* *Little Blacknose*
1931	Coatsworth	*The Cat Who Went to Heaven*
	Parrish	* *Floating Island*
	Malkus	* *The Dark Star of Itza*
	Hubbard	* *Queer Person*
	Adams	* *Mountains Are Free*
	Hewes	* *Spice and the Devil's Cave*
	Gray	* *Meggy Macintosh*
	Best	* *Garram the Hunter*
	Lide	* *Ood-Le-Uk the Wanderer*
1932	Armer	*Waterless Mountain*
	Field	* *Calico Bush*
	Lathrop	* *The Fairy Circus*
	Tietjens	* *Boy of the South Seas*
	Lownsbery	* *Out of the Flame*
	Allee	* *Jane's Island*
	Davis	* *Trace of the Wolf and Other Tales of Old Italy*
1933	Lewis	*Young Fu of the Upper Yangtze*
	Meigs	* *Swift Rivers*
	Swift	* *The Railroad to Freedom*
	Burglon	* *Children of the Soil*
1934	Meigs	*Invincible Louisa*
	Gag	* *ABC Bunny*
	Snedeker	* *The Forgotten Daughter*
	Singmaster	* *Swords of Steel*
	Berry (Best)	* *Winged Girl of Knossos*
	Schmidt	* *New Land*
	Colum	* *Big Tree of Bunlahy*
	Hewes	* *Glory of the Seas*
	Kyle	* *Apprentice of Florence*
1935	Shannon	*Dobry*
	Seeger	* *Pageant of Chinese History*
	Rourke	* *Davy Crockett*
	Stockum	* *Day on Skates*
1936	Brink	*Caddie Woodlawn*
	Seredy	* *Good Master*
	Strong	* *Honk, The Moose*
	Gray	* *Young Walter Scott*
	Sperry	* *All Sails Set: A Romance of the "Flying Cloud"*
1937	Sawyer	*Roller Skates*

Year	Author	Title
	Lenski	* *Phoebe Fairchild*
	Jones	* *Whistler's Van*
	Bemelmans	* *Golden Basket*
	Bianco	* *Winterbound*
	Rourke	* *Audubon*
	Hewes	* *The Codfish Market*
1938	Seredy	*The White Stag*
	Wilder	* *On the Banks of Plum Creek*
	Bowman	* *Pecos Bill: The Greatest Cowboy of All Time*
	Robinson	* *Bright Island*
1939	Enright	*Thimble Summer*
	Atwater	* *Mr. Popper's Penguins*
	Angelo	* *Nino*
	Crawford	* *"Hello the Boat!"*
	Eaton	* *Leader By Destiny: George Washington, Man and Patriot*
	Gray	* *Penn*
1940	Daugherty	*Daniel Boone*
	Wilder	* *By the Shores of Silver Lake*
	Seredy	* *The Singing Tree*
	Robinson	* *Runner of the Mountain Tops*
	Meader	* *Boy With a Pack*
1941	Sperry	*Call it Courage*
	Gates	* *Blue Willow*
	Wilder	* *Long Winter*
	Carr	* *Young Mac of Fort Vancouver*
	Hall	* *Nansen*
1942	Edmonds	*The Matchlock Gun*
	Wilder	* *Little Town on the Prairie*
	Foster	* *George Washington's World*
	Lenski	* *Indian Captive: The Story of Mary Jemison*
	Gaggin	* *Down Ryton Water*
1943	Gray	*Adam of the Road*
	Estes	* *The Middle Moffat*
	Hunt	* *"Have You Seen Tom Thumb?"*
1944	Forbes	*Johnny Tremain*
	Estes	* *Rufus M.*
	Sauer	* *Fog Magic*
	Wilder	* *These Happy Golden Years*
	Yates	* *Mountain Born*

Year	Author	Title
1945	Lawson	*Rabbit Hill*
	Estes	* *Hundred Dresses*
	Dalgliesh	* *The Silver Pencil*
	Foster	* *Abraham Lincoln's World*
	Eaton	* *Lone Journey: The Life of Roger Williams*
1946	Lenski	*Strawberry Girl*
	Henry	* *Justin Morgan Had a Horse*
	Means	* *The Moved-Outers*
	Weston	* *Bhimsa, The Dancing Bear*
	Shippen	* *New Found World*
1947	Bailey	*Miss Hickory*
	Barnes	* *Wonderful Year*
	Buff	* *Big Tree*
	Maxwell	* *The HeavenlyTenants*
	Fisher	* *The Avion My Uncle Flew*
	Jewett	* *The Hidden Treasure of Glaston*
1948	du Bois	*The Twenty-One Balloons*
	Courlander	* *Cow-Tail Switch and Other West African Stories*
	Bishop	* *Pancakes-Paris*
	Treffinger	* *Li Lun, Lad of Courage*
	Besterman	* *The Quaint and Curious Quest of Johnny Longfoot*
	Henry	* *Misty of Chincoteague*
1949	Henry	*King of the Wind*
	Gannett	* *My Father's Dragon*
	Holling	* *Seabird*
	Rankin	* *Daughter of the Mountains*
	Bontemps	* *Story of the Negro*
1950	de Angeli	*The Door in the Wall*
	Caudill	* *Tree of Freedom*
	Coblentz	* *The Blue Cat of Castletown*
	Montgomery	* *Kildee House*
	Foster	* *George Washington*
	Havighurst	* *Song of the Pines*
1951	Yates	*Amos Fortune, Free Man*
	Hunt	* *Better Known as Johnny Appleseed*
	Eaton	* *Gandhi, Fighter Without a Sword*
	Judson	* *Abraham Lincoln, Friend of the People*
	Parron	* *The Story of Appleby Capple*

Year	Author	Title
1952	Estes	*Ginger Pye*
	Baity	* *Americans Before Columbus*
	Holling	* *Minn of the Mississippi*
	Kalashnikoff	* *The Defender*
	Sauer	* *The Light at Tern Rocks*
	Buff	* *The Apple and the Arrow*
1953	Clark	*Secret of the Andes*
	White	* *Charlotte's Web*
	McGraw	* *Moccasin Trail*
	Weil	* *Red Sails to Capri*
	Dalgliesh	* *The Bears on Hemlock Mountain*
	Foster	* *Birthdays of Freedom*
1954	Krumgold	*. . . And Now Miguel*
	DeJong	* *Hurry Home Candy*
	Bishop	* *All Alone*
	DeJong	* *Shadrach*
	Judson	* *Theodore Roosevelt, Fighting Patriot*
	Buff	* *Magic Maize*
1955	DeJong	*The Wheel of the School*
	Dalgliesh	* *Courage of Sarah Noble*
	Ullman	* *Banner in the Sky*
1956	Latham	*Carry On, Mr.Bowditch*
	Rawlings	* *The Secret River*
	Lindquist	* *The Golden Name Day*
	Shippen	* *Men, Microscopes, and Living Things*
1957	Sorensen	*Miracles on Maple Hill*
	DeJong	* *House of Sixty Fathers*
	Gipson	* *Old Yeller*
	Judson	* *Mr. Justice Holmes*
	Rhoads	* *The Corn Grows Ripe*
	de Angeli	* *Black Fox of Lorne*
1958	Keith	*Rifles for Watie*
	Sandoz	* *The Horsecatcher*
	Enright	* *Gone-Away Lake*
	Lawson	* *The Great Wheel*
	Gurke	* *Tom Paine, Freedom's Apostle*
1959	George	*The Witch of Blackbird Pond*
	Carlson	* *The Family Under the Bridge*
	DeJong	* *Along Came a Dog*

Year	Author	Title
	Kalnay	* *Chucaro: Wild Pony of the Pampa*
	Steele	* *The Perilous Road*
1960	Krumgold	*Onion John*
	George	* *My Side of the Mountain*
	Johnson	* *America is Born*
	Kendall	* *The Gammage Cup*
1961	O'Dell	*Island of the Blue Dolphins*
	Selden	* *Cricket in Times Square*
	Johnson	* *America Moves Forward*
	Schaefer	* *Old Ramon*
1962	Speare	*The Bronze Bow*
	Tunis	* *Frontier Living*
	McGraw	* *The Golden Goblet*
	Stolz	* *Belling the Tiger*
1963	L'Engle	*A Wrinkle in Time*
	NicLeodhas	* *Thistle and Thyme: Tales and Legends from Scotland*
	Coolidge	* *Men of Athens*
1964	Neville	*It's Like This, Cat*
	North	* *Rascal*
1965	Wojciechowska	*Shadow of a Bull*
	Hunt	* *Across Five Aprils*
1966	Trevino	*I, Juan de Pareja*
	Jarrell	* *Animal Family*
	Stolz	* *Noonday Friends*
	Alexander	* *The Black Cauldron*
1967	Hunt	*Up A Road Slowly*
	Singer	* *Zlateh the Goat and Other Stories*
	O'Dell	* *The King's Fifth*
	Weik	* *The Jazz Man*
1968	Konigsburg	*From the Mixed-Up Files of Mrs. Basil E. Frankweiler*
	Snyder	* *Egypt Game*
	Konigsburg	* *Jennifer, Hecate, Macbeth, William McKinley, and Me, Elizabeth*
	O'Dell	* *The Black Pearl*
	Singer	* *The Fearsome Inn*
1969	Alexander	*The High King*
	Lester	* *To Be a Slave*

Year	Author	Title
	Singer	* *When Shlemiel Went to Warsaw and Other Stories*
1970	Armstrong	*Sounder*
	Ish-Kishor	* *Our Eddie*
	Moore	* *The Many Ways of Seeing*
	Steele	* *Journey Outside*
1971	Byars	*Summer of the Swans*
	Babbitt	* *Knee Knock Rise*
	O'Dell	* *Sing Down the Moon*
	Engdahl	* *Enchantress From the Stars*
1972	O'Brien	*Mrs. Frisby and the Rats of NIMH*
	Eckert	* *Incident At Hawk's Hill*
	Hamilton	* *Planet of Junior Brown*
	LeGuin	* *Tombs of Atuan*
	Miles	* *Annie and the Old One*
	Snyder	* *Headless Cupid*
1973	George	*Julie of the Wolves*
	Lobel	* *Frog and Toad Together*
	Reiss	* *Upstairs Room*
	Snyder	* *The Witches of Worm*
1974	Fox	*The Slave Dancer*
	Cooper	* *Dark is Rising*
1975	Hamilton	*M.C. Higgins, The Great*
	Collier	* *My Brother Sam is Dead*
	Greene	* *Philip Hall Likes Me, I Reckon Maybe*
	Pope	* *The Perilous Gard*
	Raskin	* *Figgs and Phantoms*
1976	Cooper	*The Grey King*
	Mathis	* *Hundred Penny Box*
	Yep	* *Dragon Wings*
1977	Taylor	*Roll of Thunder, Hear My Cry*
	Bond	* *String in the Harp*
	Steig	* *Abel's Island*
1978	Paterson	*Bridge to Terabithia*
	Cleary	* *Ramona and Her Father*
	Highwater	* *Anpao: An American Indian Odyssey*
1979	Raskin	*The Westing Game*
	Paterson	* *Great Gilly Hopkins*

Year	Author	Title
1980	Blos	*A Gathering of Days*
	Kherdian	* *Road From Home*
1981	Paterson	*Jacob Have I Loved*
	Langton	* *Fledgling*
	L'Engle	* *Ring of Endless Light*
1982	Willard	*A Visit to William Blake's Inn*
	Cleary	* *Ramona Quimby*
	Siegal	* *Upon the Head of the Goat*
1983	Voigt	*Dicey's Song*
	Fleischman	* *Graven Images*
	Fritz	* *Homesick: My Own Story*
	Hamilton	* *Sweet Whispers, Brother Rush*
	McKinley	* *Blue Sword*
	Steig	* *Dr. De Soto*
1984	Cleary	*Dear Mr. Henshaw*
	Brittain	* *Wish Giver*
	Lasky	* *Sugaring Time*
	Speare	* *Sign of the Beaver*
	Voigt	* *Solitary Blue*
1985	McKinley	*The Hero and the Crown*
	Brooks	* *The Moves Make the Man*
	Fox	* *One-Eyed Cat*
	Jukes	* *Like Jake and Me*
1986	Maclachlan	*Sarah, Plain and Tall*
	Blumberg	* *Commodore Perry in the Land of the Shogun*
	Paulsen	* *Dogsong*
1987	Fleischman	*Whipping Boy*
	Bauer	* *On My Honor*
	Lauber	* *Volcano*
	Rylant	* *Fine White Dust*
1988	Freedman	*Lincoln: A Photobiography*
	Mazer	* *After the Rain*
	Paulsen	* *Hatchet*
1989	Fleischman	*Joyfeel Noise: Poems for Two Voices*
	Hamilton	* *In the Beginning*
	Meyers	* *Scorpions*
1990	Lawry	*Number the Stars*
	Lisle	* *Afternoon of the Elves*

Year	Author	Title
	Paulsen	* *Winter Room*
	Stapler	* *Shahann*
1991	Spinelli	*Maniac Magce*
	Ani	* *The True Confessions of Charlotte Doyle*
1992	Neylar	*Shiloh*

The Caldecott Medal

The Caldecott Medal is awarded annually by the Association for Library Service to Children, a division of the American Library Association. In 1938, the first Caldecott Medal, which was donated by Frederic G. Melcher (1879-1963) of the R. R. Bowker Company, was awarded to the artist of the most distinguished American picture book for children published in the United States during the preceding year. The name of Randolph Caldecott, the famous English illustrator of books for children, was chosen for the medal because his work best represented "joyousness of picture books as well as their beauty." The horseman on the medal is taken from one of his illustrations for John Gilpin.

Caldecott Medal Books

*denotes Caldecott Honor Book

Year	Author	Title
1938	Fish	*Animals of the Bible*
	Artzybasheff	* *Seven Simeons: A Russian Tale*
		* *Four and Twenty Blackbirds*
1939	Handforth	*Mei Li*
	Daugherty	* *Andy and the Lion*
	Armer	* *The Forest Pool*
	Leaf	* *Wee Gillis*
	Newberry	* *Barkis*
	Gag	* *Snow White and the Seven Dwarfs*
1940	d'Aulaire	*Abraham Lincoln*
	Bemelmans	* *Madeline*
	Hader	* *Cock-A-Doodle-Doo*
	Ford	* *The Ageless Story*
1941	Lawson	*They Were Strong and Good*
	Newberry	* *April's Kittens*

Year	Author	Title
1942	McCloskey	*Make Way for Ducklings*
	Holling	* *Paddle-To-The-Sea*
	Petersham	* *An American ABC*
	Clark	* *In My Mother's House*
	Gag	* *Nothing at All*
1943	Burton	*The Little House*
	Buff	* *Dash and Dart*
	Newberry	* *Marshmallow*
1944	Thurber	*Many Moons*
	Brown	* *A Child's Good Night Book*
	Kingman	* *Pierre Pigeon*
	Hader	* *The Mighty Hunter*
	Chan	* *Good-Luck Horse*
	Jones	* *Small Rain: Verses from the Bible*
1945	Field	*Prayer for a Child*
	de Angeli	* *Yonie Wondernose*
	Ets	* *In the Forest*
	Tudor	* *Mother Goose*
	Sawyer	* *The Christmas Anna Angel*
1946	Petersham	*The Rooster Crows*
	Reyher	* *My Mother Is the Most Beautiful Woman in the World*
	Brown	* *Little Lost Lamb*
	Wheeler	* *Sing Mother Goose*
	Wiese	* *You Can Write Chinese*
1947	MacDonald	*The Little Island*
	Tresselt	* *Rain Drop Splash*
	Flack	* *Boats on the River*
	Graham	* *Timothy Turtle*
	Poloti	* *Pedro, The Angel of Olvera Street*
	Wheeler	* *Sing in Praise: A Collection of the Best Loved Hymns*
1948	Tresselt	*White Snow, Bright Snow*
	Brown	* *Stone Soup*
	Seuss	* *McElligot's Pool*
	Schreiber	* *Bambino the Clown*
	Davis	* *Roger and the Fox*
	Malcolmson	* *Song of Robin Hood*
1949	Hader	*The Big Show*
	McCloskey	* *Blueberries for Sal*

Year	Author	Title
	McGinley	* *All Around the Town*
	Politi	* *Juanita*
	Wiese	* *Fish in the Air*
1950	Politi	*Song of the Swallows*
	Krauss	* *The Happy Day*
	Seuss	* *Bartholomew and the Oobleck*
	Holbrook	* *America's Ethan Allen*
	Davis	* *The Wild Birthday Cake*
	Brown	* *Henry Fisherman*
1951	Milhous	*The Egg Tree*
	Brown	* *Dick Whittington and His Cat*
	Seuss	* *If I Ran the Zoo*
	Lipkind	* *The Two Reds*
	Newberry	* *T-Bone, The Baby-Sitter*
	McGinley	* *The Most Wonderful Doll in the World*
1952	Lipkind	*Finders Keepers*
	Brown	* *Skipper John's Cook*
	Ets	* *Mr. T. W. Anthony Woo*
1953	Ward	*The Biggest Bear*
	McCloskey	* *One Morning in Maine*
	Zolotow	* *The Storm Book*
	Perrault	* *Puss In Boots*
	Kepes	* *Five Little Monkeys*
	Eichenberg	* *Ape in a Cape: An Alphabet of Odd Animals*
1954	Bemelmans	*Madeline's Rescue*
	Krauss	* *A Very Special House*
	Sawyer	* *Journey Cake, Ho!*
	Schlein	* *When Will the World Be Mine?*
	Andersen	* *The Steadfast Tin Soldier*
	Birnbaum	* *Green Eyes*
1955	Brown	*Cinderella, or the Little Glass Slipper*
	Brown	* *Wheel on the Chimney*
	Dalgleish	* *The Thanksgiving Story*
	de Angeli	* *Book of Nursery and Mother Goose Rhymes*
1956	Langstaff	*Frog Went A-Courtin'*
	Ets	* *Play With Me*
	Yashima	* *Crow Boy*
1957	Udry	*A Tree is Nice*
	DuBois	* *Lion*
	Tudor	* *1 is One*

Year	Author	Title
	Ets	* Mister Penny's Race Horse
	Titus	* Anatole
	Elkin	* Gillespie and the Guards
1958	McCloskey	Time of Wonder
	Freeman	* Fly High, Fly Low
	Titus	* Anatole and the Cat
1959	Cooney	* Chanticleer and the Fox
	Joslin	* What Do You Say, Dear?
	Yashima	* Umbrella
	Frasconi	* The House That Jack Built: La Maison Que Jacques a Batie
1960	Ets	Nine Days to Christmas
	Goudey	* Houses from the Sea
	Udry	* The Moon Jumpers
1961	Robbins	Baboushka and the Three Kings
	Lionni	* Inch By Inch
1962	Brown	Once a Mouse
	Minarik	* Little Bear's Visit
	Spier	* The Fox Went Out on a Chilly Night
	Goudey	* The Day We Saw the Sun Come Up
1963	Keats	The Snowy Day
	Zolotow	* Mr. Rabbit and the Lovely Present
	Belting	* The Sun Is a Golden Earring
1964	Sendak	Where the Wild ThingsAre
	Lionni	* Swimmy
	Leodhas	* All in the Morning Early Mother Goose and Nursery Rhymes
1965	de Regniers	May I Bring a Friend?
	Caudill	* A Pocketful of Cricket
	Scheer	* Rain Makes Applesauce
	Hodges	* The Wave
1966	Leodhas	Always Room for One More
	Ets	* Just Me
	Tresselt	* Hide and Seek Fog
		* Tom Tit Tot: An English Folktale
1967	Ness	Sam, Bangs and Moonshine
	Emberley	* One Wide River to Cross
1968	Emberley	Drummer Hoff
	Lionni	* Frederick

Year	Author	Title
	Yolen	* *The Emperor and the Kite*
	Yashima	* *Seashore Story*
1969	Ransome	*The Fool of the World and the Flying Ship*
	Dayrell	* *Why the Sun and the Moon Live in the Sky*
1970	Steig	*Sylvester and the Magic Pebble*
	Keats	* *Goggles*
	Lionni	* *Alexander and the Wind-Up Mouse*
	Turkle	* *Thy Friend, Obadiah*
	Zemach	* *The Judge: An Untrue Tale*
	Preston	* *Pop Corn and Ma Goodness*
1971	Haley	*A Story a Story*
	Lobel	* *Frog and Toad Are Friends*
	Sendak	* *In the Night Kitchen*
	Sleator	* *The Angry Moon*
1972	Hogrogian	*One Fine Day*
	Domanska	* *If All the Seas Were One*
	Feelings	* *Moja Means One*
	Ryan	* *Hildilid's Night*
1973	Mosel	*The Funny Little Woman*
	Baylor	* *When Clay Sings*
	Jarrell	* *Snow White and the Seven Dwarfs*
	McDermott	* *Anansi the Spider*
	Baskin	* *Hosie's Alphabet*
1974	Zemach	*Duffy and the Devil*
	Macaulay	* *Cathedral*
	Jeffers	* *Three Jovial Huntsmen*
1975	McDermott	*Arrow to the Sun*
	Feelings	* *Jambo Means Hello*
1976	Aardema	*Why Mosquitoes Buzz in People's Ears*
	Baylor	* *The Desert is Theirs*
	DePaola	* *Strega Nona*
1977	Musgrove	*Ashanti To Zulu*
	Baylor	* *Hawk, I'm Your Brother*
	Hogrogian	* *The Contest*
	Steig	* *The Amazing Bone*
	McDermott	* *The Golem*
	Goffstein	* *Fish for Supper*
1978	Spier	*Noah's Ark*
	Macaulay	* *Castle*

Year	Author	Title
	Zemach	* *It Could Always Be Worse*
1979	Goble	*The Girl Who Loved Wild Horses*
	Baylor	* *The Way to Start a Day*
	Crews	* *Freight Train*
1980	Hall	*Ox-Cart Man*
	Isadora	* *Ben's Trumpet*
	Shulevitz	* *The Treasure*
	Van Allsburg	* *The Garden of Abdul Gasazi*
1981	Lobel	*Fables*
	Bang	* *The Grey Lady and the Strawberry Snatcher*
	Crews	* *Truck*
	Low	* *Mice Twice*
	Plume	* *The Bremen Town Musicians*
1982	Van Allsburg	*Jumanji*
	Baker	* *Where the Buffaloes Begin*
	Lobel	* *On Market Street*
	Sendak	* *Outside Over There*
	Willard	* *A Visit to William Blake's Inn*
1983	Cendrars	*Shadow*
	Rylant	* *When I Was Young in the Mountains*
	Williams	* *A Chair for My Mother*
1984	Provenson	*The Glorious Flight*
	Bang	* *Ten, Nine, Eight*
	Hyman	* *Little Red Riding Hood*
1985	Hodges	*Saint George and the Dragon*
	Lesser	* *Hansel and Gretel*
	Steptoe	* *The Story of Jumping Mouse*
	Tafuri	* *Have You Seen My Duckling?*
1986	Van Allsburg	*The Polar Express*
	Rylant	* *The Relatives Came*
	Wood	* *King Bidgood's in the Bathtub*
1987	Yorinks	*Hey, Al*
	Grifalconi	* *The Village of Round and Square Houses*
	MacDonald	* *Alphabatics*
	Zelinsky	* *Rumpelstiltskin*
1988	Yolen	*Own Moon*
	Steptoe	* *Mufaro's Beautiful Daughters*

Year	Author	Title
1989	Ackerman	*Song and Dance Man*
	Marshall	* *Goldilocks and the Three Bears*
	McKissack	* *Mirandy and Brother Wind*
	Snyder	* *The Boy of the Three-Year Nap*
	Wiesner	* *Free Fall*
1990	Young	*Lon Po Po*
	Ehlert	* *Color Zoo*
	Kimmel	* *Hershel and the Hanukkah Goblins*
	Peet	* *Bill Peet: An Autobiography*
	San Souci	* *The Talking Eggs*
1991	Macaulay	*Black and White*
	Williams	*More More More Said the Baby*

Children's Choices for 1992
A project of the International Reading
Association and the Children's Book Council

What is Children's Choices?

Each year, 10,000 children from five regions of the United States mark their ballots yes, no, or maybe in response to their teacher's question, "Do you like this book?" Children's Choices 1992 is the result of the careful selection by these children of newly published trade books they enjoyed. This list is designed for use not only by teachers, librarians, and administrators, but also by parents, grandparents, care-givers, and anyone who wishes to encourage young people to read for pleasure.

What Does the Information in the Annotations Mean?

Books selected for the Children's Choices list have been grouped by these reading levels:

All ages

Beginning independent reading

Younger readers (ages 5-8)

Middle grades (ages 8-10)

Older readers (ages 10-13)

Many books easily read by primary readers are enjoyed by more advanced readers, and many titles for older readers are accessible to younger readers or can be read aloud in the classroom.

All Ages

An Alphabet of Rotten Kids! David Elliott. Illustrated by Oscar de Mejo.

> The alphabet will never seem the same after you read this book. Meet Horatio, who stuffs his mouth with frozen peas, then sneezes. Or Bartholomew, who pours ink into his teacher's tea and turns her lips blue. These twenty-six poems are about some of the most rotten, mischievous, uncontrollable children you will ever meet. The students will love them.

The Australian Echidna. Eleanor Stodard. Illustrated with color photographs.

> The life cycle of the amazing and unusual Australian echidna, or anteater, is told with an easily understandable, fact-filled text, and more than forty dramatic color photographs.

The Big Green Book. Fred Pearce. Illustrated by Ian Winton.

> Realistic, factual, and thorough, this book shows, by catchy chapter titles but a matter-of-fact tone, how humans affect the earth, especially today. Included is a list of books, magazines, and organizations that tell us what we need to help our earth.

Christmas in July. Arthur Yorinks. Illustrated by Richard Egielski.

> Townspeople were prepared for Santa's visit. However, Santa was unable to make his deliveries because his pants were lost at the dry cleaners. Santa's attempts to rescue his pants make a good, comical Christmas read. A second-grader exclaimed, "This book should get a '10.' "

The Frog Prince Continued. Jon Scieszka. Illustrated by Steve Johnson.

> A delightful and humorous sequel in which the Prince and Princess find out the shocking truth about life "happily ever after." All ages will enjoy this book.

Gobble! The Complete Book of Thanksgiving Words. Lynda Graham-Barber. Illustrated by Betsy Lewin.

> "A book for fun and information," wrote one seventh-grader. Each custom or food related to Thanksgiving is explored in detail. An American history trivia book.

Hey, Hay! A Wagonful of Funny Homonym Riddles. Marvin Terban. Illustrated by Kevin Hawkes.

> "These riddles are fun," exclaimed a third-grader when this homonyn

riddle book was read aloud. The answers are all homonyms—sometimes two, three, and even four words that sound the same.

It Was A Dark and Stormy Night. Keith Moseley. Illustrated by Linda Birkinshaw.

Jack and the Beanstalk. Retold by Steven Kellogg. Ilustrated by the author.

> This rich retelling of the popular tale, featuring Kellogg's magical, often humorous illustrations, has universal appeal. As one class commented, "We think Mr. Kellogg is a great artist."

Knock! Knock! Colin and Jacqui Hawkins. Illustrated by Colin Hawkins.

> "Who's there?" or "What's there?" Thrills, chills, and laughter await readers of all ages as they guess what creature lurks behind the door.

The Man Behind the Magic: The Story of Walt Disney. Katherine and Richard Greene. Illustrated with photographs.

> Walt Disney was not afraid to work hard and make his dreams become a reality. This book contains many interesting quotes by Disney and is a very descriptive biography.

Mistakes That Worked. Charlotte Foltz Jones. Illustrated by John O'Brien.

> The who, what, where, when, and how of things we use each day that started out as mistakes, like doughnuts, popsicles, and Coca-Cola. Kids learn that making a mistake is a learning experience.

Not the Piano, Mrs. Medley! Evan Levine. Illustrated by S.D. Schindler.

> "It's like my Mom camping," commented one young child. Mrs. Medley just cannot seem to leave anything at home as she prepares to go to the beach. Once at the seashore she forgets all about those "necessities."

The Old Ladies Who Liked Cats. Carol Greene. Illustrated by Loretta Krupinski.

> Mutual need is the theme of this book that describes how some old ladies saved the town by letting their cats out at night. This funny story deals with the balance in nature and will be enjoyed by all.

Somebody Loves You, Mr. Hatch. Eileen Spinelli. Illustrated by Paul Yalowitz.

> A sad, lonely man becomes enlightened when a special gift is sent to him. This story shows the importance of friendship in everyone's life.

A Southern Time Christmas. Robert Bernardini. Illustrated by James Rice.

> Students enjoy this hilarious regional take-off on the traditional Christmas poem, "T'was the Night Before Christmas." Jed, Santa's elf, gives special insights into customs that are uniquely Southern. A good read aloud.

Tailypo! Retold by Jan Wahl. Illustrated by Wil Clay.

> A wonderful African-American folktale told by an old man to the author:

Why never to chase with a hatchet a creature that has a long, long tail, and is crawling through your wall.

Walt Disney's 101 Dalmatians: Illustrated Classic. Adapted from the film by Ann Braybrooks. Illustrated by Gil DiCicco.

Newlywed Dalmatians and their human "pets" take you on an adventure as their family stretches from fifteen puppies to become a plantation for 101 Dalmatians. This story is filled with suspense and beautiful illustrations. A book to be shared by the whole family.

Whales. Gail Gibbons. Illustrated by the author.

This well-illustrated, factual book on the lives of many different whales easily piques curiosity and raises questions for discussion. "I didn't know..." is a comment often heard.

When I Was Your Age. Ken Adams. Illustrated by Val Biro.

"That's just what my Grandpa says," was one comment overheard when a teacher read aloud this delightful book about Sammy and his boastful Grandpa, who had things much worse when he was a boy. Val Biro's illustrations are hilarious.

Wind in the Long Grass: A Collection of Haiku. Edited by William J. Higginson. Illustrated by Sandra Speidel.

An international collection with illustrations as gently evocative as haiku itself. Children commented, "The beautiful pictures made me feel peaceful." A brief description of haiku's structure encourages youngsters to try their hand at this ancient poetic form.

Window on the Deep: The Adventures of Underwater Explorer Sylvia Earle. Andrea Conley. Illustrated with photographs.

This book is a wonderful way to learn about scuba diving and ocean life. Beautiful photographs and detailed illustrations.

A Young Painter: The Life and Paintings of Wang Yani—China's Extraordinary Young Artist. Zheng Zhensun and Alice Low. Illustrated with photographs and reproductions.

The life and works of Wang Yani, a Chinese girl who starts painting at age three in China. Many beautiful color photographs of her monkeys, lions, cranes, peacocks, and landscape paintings.

Beginning Independent Reading

Five Little Monkeys Sitting in a Tree. Eileen Christelow. Illustrated by the author.

A humorous, familiar tale of five monkeys who tease a crocodile. One second-grader commented, "It's good because it repeats, and you get to know the words."

The Happy Hippopotami. Bill Martin, Jr. Illustrated by Betsy Everitt.

A happy hippo adventure to the beach filled with colorful pictures and creative language that invites the reader to participate. You will want to join the hilarious hippopotami for a hip-hippo celebration next year.

Happy Thanksgiving Rebus. David A. Adler. Illustrated by Jan Palmer.

This story within a story is enriched by rebus pictures and detailed illustrations. The story of the first Thanksgiving helps a modern boy learn the real meaning of sharing.

If Dinosaurs Came to Town. Dom Mansell. Illustrated by the author.

What would it be like if dinosaurs were still alive and roaming around your town? What would they be like? Where would they live? Would you be safe? Read this book and you will find out.

In a Cabin in a Wood. Adapted by Darcie McNally. Illustrated by Robin Michal Koontz.

A colorful story from the song, "In a Cabin in a Wood." A rabbit comes up with a clever solution that helps an old man. Very detailed illustrations.

In the Tall, Tall Grass. Denise Fleming. Illustrated by the author.

Catchy, rhyming words in big print skip and dip across the pages of this read-aloud book. It is a book to share, with bright illustrations as insects and grassy creatures are revealed. Children ask, "What's next?"

Matthew's Dream. Leo Lionni. Illustrated by the author.

Matthew does not know what he wants to be when he grows up. A trip to the museum helps him decide, and his dreary world becomes a bright and colorful one.

My Friend Whale. Simon James. Illustrated by the author.

Simple words and delightful pictures tell the story of a boy's friendship with a blue whale. Along the way, the reader learns facts about whales and their fragile environment.

Piggies. Don Wood and Audrey Wood. Illustrated by Don Wood.

A new twist on "This Little Piggy Goes to Market." The Woods have real little pigs on ten fingers, and the pigs are fat, smart, long, silly, and wee. They are usually good, but at bedtime they dance on your toes.

Sheep in a Shop. Nancy Shaw. Illustrated by Margot Apple.

Can you imagine seeing some silly sheep on a birthday shopping spree with no money? This wonderfully illustrated book "sheds" some shear delight on a silly sheepish solution to their problems.

Super Cluck. Jane O'Connor and Robert O'Connor. Illustrated by Megan Lloyd.

> A big, strong chick from another planet has trouble making friends with the other chickens. But during a heroic act, he proves he is not a wimp or dumb chick after all.

Walt Disney's 101 Dalmatians: A Counting Book. Fran Manushkin. Illustrated by Russell Hicks.

> Out for a walk, ninety-nine puppies are frightened by a firetruck and run in all directions. Young readers count from one to one-hundred-and-one while finding the missing puppies on each page. A real favorite of kindergartners and first-graders.

Young Readers

An Alligator Named . . . Alligator. Lois G. Grambling. Illustrated by Doug Cushman.

> A little boy's desire for a pet alligator turns into an unusual surprise for his family and neighbors. What do you do with an alligator in the house?

Appalachia: The Voices of Sleeping Birds. Cynthia Rylant. Illustrated by Barry Moser.

> A short, easy-to-read book about the Appalachian Mountain people growing up and living in coal mining areas.

Arthur Meets the President. Marc Brown. Illustrated by the author.

> Arthur wins an essay contest and is off with his classmates to attend a ceremony at the White House. When he forgets his speech, he gets some unexpected help in this fifteenth book in the humorous Arthur Adventure series.

Christopher Columbus: From Vision to Voyage. Joan Anderson. Illustrated with photographs by George Ancona.

> Columbus, an ordinary man who had the sea in his veins and dreams in his head, changed people's view of the world forever. Anderson and Ancona bring history excitingly to life as they reveal the inner journey that led to Columbus's first sailing in 1492.

Clifford, We Love You. Norman Bridwell. Illustrated by the author.

> For twenty-five years, Emily Elizabeth and her big red dog, Clifford, have delighted boys and girls. But now Clifford feels blue. Nothing cheers him up until Emily Elizabeth decides to write a happy song. Words and music are included.

Cranberries. William Jaspersohn. Illustrated with photographs by the author.

> An informative account of how cranberries are grown, harvested, and

distributed. This detailed text of a native American fruit is enhanced by vivid photographs and enjoyed by all ages.

Dear Mr. Blueberry. Simon James. Illustrated by the author.

An engaging story of a girl who imagines there is a whale in her pond. She exchanges letters with her teacher, who tries to convince her a whale could not live in a pond. Through their correspondence, we learn facts about whales.

Dinostory. Michaela Morgan. Illustrated by True Kelley.

Andrew Gilmore is crazy about dinosaurs. On his birthday, he makes his wish known to a wizard, who makes many dinosaurs appear. Andrew discovers that dinosaurs are not that much fun.

The Dog Who Had Kittens. Polly Robertus. Illustrated by Janet Stevens.

Baxter, the Bassett hound, lifts his head and howls, thinking, "Just what I need, more cats around the place." But he soon begins spending all his time with the kittens, until one day he discovers their box empty. Stevens' illustrations capture the humor and sentiment in this favorite of first-graders.

For Laughing Out Loud: Poems to Tickle Your Funnybone. Selected by Jack Prelutsky. Illustrated by Marjorie Priceman.

Just as the title suggests, Prelutsky has collected a book of poems to "tickle your funnybone." Humorous poems by an array of American writers. Contains author and title indexes.

Fritz and the Mess Fairy. Rosemary Wells. Illustrated by the author.

Not only is Fritz so messy that he cannot find things in his own room, he creates difficulties for his sisters and parents. After a visit from the "mess fairy," who was even sloppier than Fritz, he decides to change his ways—almost.

Frog Medicine. Mark Teague. Illustrated by the author.

A boy named Elmo finds himself stuck doing a report on a book called "Frog Medicine." Worse, he begins turning into a frog. By traveling to Frogtown, he learns valuable lessons about frogs, homework, and life. Some second-graders surmised that "If you don't do your work, you'll get the big 'F', frog legs."

The Grumpalump. Sarah Hayes. Illustrated by Barbara Firth.

Rhythm and rhyme, in "The House That Jack Built" tradition, combine with a surprise ending to delight young readers. Just what is a grumpalump? The guessing game can continue page by page.

Henry's Wild Morning. Margaret Greaves. Illustrated by Teresa O'Brien.

The runt of the litter and the only striped kitten, Henry imagines he is a fierce tiger and has a wild and mischievous adventure. Bold and colorful illustrations made this a favorite of first- and second-graders.

The Holiday Handwriting School. Robin Pulver. Illustrated by G. Brian Karas.

Santa, Tooth Fairy, and Easter Bunny experience difficulty with their handwriting. Mrs. Holiday offers personal advice and, in return, receives loving mementos from her special students. One reader commented, "Mrs. Holiday was nice because she helped them to write." Others enjoyed the happy ending.

If You Give a Moose a Muffin. Laura Joffe Numeroff. Illustrated by Felicia Bond.

This circular tale is a comic sequel to "If You Give A Mouse A Cookie." The much larger moose creates some hilarious situations when he visits a young boy and eats all the muffins.

Jeremy's Tail. Duncan Ball. Illustrated by Donna Rawlins.

An entertaining book about Jeremy's travels around the world trying to pin the tail on a donkey that was in his own house. The illustrations show various parts of the world and stress determination.

John F. Kennedy: Young People's President. Catherine Corley Anderson. Illustrated with photographs.

The life and times of President John Fitzgerald Kennedy, who grew up in a large Irish family in Boston, Mass. Children can relate to the manner in which this story is told.

King of the Playground. Phyllis Reynolds Naylor. Illustrated by Nola Langner Malone.

Kevin is afraid of Sammy, who has declared himself "King of the Playground." After several talks with his father, Kevin has the courage to confront the bully. The story lends itself to discussions of courage and problem-solving.

Max's Dragon Shirt. Rosemary Wells. Illustrated by the author.

Follow Max and Ruby shopping in a department store. Max's determination to get a dragon shirt leads him away from the distracted sister and into trouble. A hilarious read-aloud romp.

Mona the Vampire. Sonia Holleyman. Illustrated by the author.

The outlandish antics of Mona and her cat, Fang, disrupt school and ballet class as she pretends to be a vampire. Mona keeps the reader eager to see what she will do next.

The Moon Clock. Matt Faulkner. Illustrated by the author.

In this fantasy, a little girl stays home from school because the other children tease her. A captain from a different place enters her room through her toy chest and cheers her on to brave deeds. The illustrations are wonderful.

Mucky Moose. Jonathan Allen. Illustrated by the author.

Mucky, the muckiest, smelliest moose that ever lived, is pursued by the biggest wolf in the forest, and he is extra hungry. Humorous illustrations depict the wolf's attempts to eat Mucky. The outcome is unexpected.

No Plain Pets! Marc Ian Barasch. Illustrated by Henrik Drescher.

Will an ordinary pet cat, dog, or pony do? A young boy's fancy for a pet is vividly displayed in color and rhyme as he soars and sails using his imagination searching for the right pet.

Polar Bear, Polar Bear, What Do You Hear? Bill Martin Jr. Illustrated by Eric Carle.

Do you know the sounds that the two thousand animals make? The animals hear each other growling, snorting, and hissing, and the zookeeper hears the children imitating the animals. A wonderful chant-along book.

Rosie's Baby Tooth. Maryann Macdonald. Illustrated by Melissa Sweet.

Rosie is not sure she likes losing a baby tooth and then giving it to the Tooth Fairy, so she writes to the Tooth Fairy. The letter she receives convinces Rosie that losing baby teeth can be special after all.

Ruby the Copycat. Peggy Rathmann. Illustrated by the author.

This is a charming, humorous, sensitive tale about self-identification. Everywhere children are searching for acceptance and approval. With the help of Miss Hart, her teacher, Ruby realizes her own worth.

Sea Squares. Joy N. Hulme. Illustrated by Carol Schwartz.

Counting and multiplication facts are discovered with playful rhymes featuring ocean creatures such as "four slippery seals, with four flippers each . . . (making) sixteen flippery feet." The pictures and border designs complete the watery scene.

Seven Little Hippos. Mike Thaler. Illustrated by Jerry Smath.

A delightful, predictable book. Children recognize the similarity to the familiar "Five Little Monkeys" rhyme. The surprise raucous ending after the doctor leaves will thrill children of all ages.

Siegfried. Diane Stanley. Illustrated by John Sandford.

Cat lovers will feel at home with Siegfried, a very old cat who has difficulty adapting to the sound of the cuckoo clock that enters his home one Christmas. The illustrations are warm and inviting, and set the mood.

Some Birthday. Patricia Polacco. Illustrated by the author.

Patricia is concerned that her father forgot her birthday. This well-written and illustrated story describes the scariest and most exciting birthdays anyone could have.

Take Time to Relax. Nancy Carlson. Illustrated by the author.

What does a busy family do when it becomes snowbound? Tina, her mom, and her dad are always rushing from one activity to another. They learn that being home can also be fun.

That's Good! That's Bad! Margery Cuyler. Illustrated by David Catrow.

Children learn to expect the unexpected in this vividly illustrated tale. A little boy's adventure (That's Good!) and misadventure (That's Bad!) with his jungle friends are told in an appealingly repetitive pattern that children love.

Where's That Bus? Eileen Brown. Illustrated by the author.

Two friends, Rabbit and Mole, try to catch a bus to visit Squirrel. While waiting for the bus, Rabbit and Mole get distracted and do not see the buses that pass. Where is that bus? Just wait and see.

Who Are You? John Schindel. Illustrated by James Watts.

"You are too little, too small, too young . . ." are unwelcome words to children's ears. Brown Bear's parents wisely allow him to discover for himself that it is much more fun to be Brown Bear than to be a grownup.

Middle Grades

The A-to-Z Book of Cars. Angela Royston. Illustrated by Terry Pastor.

"Mint." That is what a group of sixth-graders said after reading this book. This illustrated alphabet book of cars starts with Alfa Romeo and ends with the Zodiac Zephyr. A must read for all car buffs.

Alligators to Zooplankton: A Dictionary of Water Babies. Les Kaufman and the staff of the New England Aquarium. Illustrated with photographs.

An A-to-Z book with fascinating information and photographs about aquatic animals and their young. Lots of information and many unusual stories about different ways that life begins in the water.

American Tall Tales. Mary Pope Osborne. Illustrated with wood engravings by Michael McCurdy.

A superb collection of America's first folk heroes, including Davy Crockett, Paul Bunyan, Sally Ann Thunder, Ann Whirlwind, and six other unique characters. Sure to make you laugh. Historical notes give background about each character.

Best Enemies Again. Kathleen Leverich. Illustrated by Walter Lorraine.

> Felicity Doll is back, this time to challenge Priscilla in the lemonade business. And when poor speller Priscilla gets a "study buddy" to help her, it is none other than Felicity, the snake. The rivalry continues in this humorous, easy chapter book.

Bingo. Adapted by Beth Goodman. Illustrated with photographs.

> Children are enchanted with Bingo, an amazing and helpful dog. After leaving the circus, he rescues Chuckie from a burning building, helps capture robbers, and meets other challenges. "Bingo is a real hero," said a fourth-grader. "I wish he were my dog."

Discovering Christopher Columbus: How History is Invented. Kathy Pelta. Illustrated with photographs.

> This book not only explores the story of Christopher Columbus, but also delves into the research process. It takes a historical look at information to try to determine fact.

Earthquake. Christopher Lampton.

> General information about earthquakes and specific attention to the San Francisco earthquakes of 1906 and 1989 provide description about the dangers of earthquakes. One fourth-grade class agreed that the pictures were colorful, real, and showed action.

Fourth-Grade Rats. Jerry Spinelli. Illustrated by Paul Casale.

> "I wouldn't want to turn into a rat," wrote one fourth-grader. An appealing story for intermediate students about growing up and peer pressure. "A funny book that's easy to read," said another fourth-grader.

George Washington: The Man Who Would Not Be King. Stephen Krensky. Illustrations from various sources.

> Imagine this change in history—King George of America. This book is the story of a man popular enough to have been chosen king, but wise enough to refuse.

The Kite that Braved Old Orchard Beach. X.J. Kennedy. Illustrated by Marian Young.

> This book of poems spans the years of growing up and the special days in each year, and it captures the thoughts of children. Great lines: "With things that matter to me, not for sale at any price."

The Last Princess: The Story of Princess Ka'iulani of Hawai'i. Fay Stanley. Illustrated by Diane Stanley.

> Young readers will admire Princess Ka'iulani, the last heir to the Hawaiian throne, who fought bravely to preserve the rights of her people during a

time of heartbreaking change. Full-page illustrations enhance this bitter-sweet story of a princess who could never be queen.

Macmillan Animal Encyclopedia for Children. Roger Few. Illustrated with full-color drawings and photographs.

"What I like about this book is that it shows all the animals that live in certain areas, like mountains, woods, deserts and oceans," commented a fifth-grader. Arranged by natural habitat, this book explores the creatures that live in each and why.

Make Four Million Dollar$ by Next Thur$day. Stephen Manes. Illustrated by George Ulrich.

When Jason finds the book, "Make Four Millions Dollar$ by Next Thur$day," he is determined to follow the zany advice of the author, Dr. K. Pinkerton Silverfish. Will he become four million dollars richer? More importantly, can you?

Manatee: On Location. Kathy Darling. Photographs by Tara Darling.

The large grass-eating mammal called the manatee is a slowly vanishing species. Photographs give the reader a bird's-eye view of life under the sea with the manatee. The text is concise and easy to read.

The Moon of the Alligator. Jean Craighead George. Illustrated by Michael Rothman.

An addition to "The Thirteen Moons" series, this book describes the ecosystem of the Florida Everglades by telling the story of one alligator and her search for food as the dry season begins. Lyrical prose and superb wildlife illustrations.

The Moon of the Gray Wolves. Jean Craighead George. Illustrated by Sal Catalano.

This is one for the animal lovers. Children enjoy the author's storylike way of describing the life of the gray wolf in Alaska.

The Moon of the Mountain Lions. Jean Craighead George. Illustrated by Ron Parker.

Patterned after a Native American folktale of night animals, this story shows us the mountain lion in Washington state, but describes many animals of that region and their habits. An easy narrative style incorporates ecology and the balance of nature.

Nine O'Clock Lullaby. Marilyn Singer. Illustrated by France Lessac.

Rich language and beautiful illustrations make this story about time zones and distant lands an excellent choice for language arts and content areas. A useful interdisciplinary addition.

Of Swans, Sugarplums, and Satin Slippers: Ballet Stories for Children. Violette Verdy. Illustrated by Marcia Brown.

A short summary precedes each of six classical ballet stories containing magic, and the themes of good and evil. Beautiful watercolors.

175 More Science Experiments to Amuse and Amaze Your Friends. Terry Cash, Steve Parker, and Barbara Taylor. Illustrated by Kuo Kang Chen and Peter Bull.

"You should get this book and try some of the tricks. I did," one fifth-graders commented. A sequel to "Experiments to Amuse and Amaze Your Friends," this book contains a variety of illustrated, concise experiments on sound, electricity, simple chemistry, and weather.

One World. Michael Foreman. Illustrated by the author.

Creating a microcosm from a tidal pool, children gradually see the delicate balance between humans and the environment. One third-grader commented, "It is a good book to remind people that we only have one world and we need to take care of it."

Pearl Harbor! Wallace B. Black and Jean F. Blashfield.

Actual photographs enhance this well-written text about this major historical event. This book makes history come alive.

The River. Gary Paulsen.

This is a must read for anyone who traveled with Brian Robeson on his terrifying adventures in the book, "Hatchet." Two years after Brian's first encounter with the wilderness, the government asks him to do it all again so others may learn from his survival techniques.

Shadow Theater: Games and Projects. Denny Robson and Vanessa Bailey. Illustrated with drawings and photographs.

A great book for students who want to use their imagination and creativity. Good collection of ways to make shadow characters come alive. Describes types of hand shadows, and includes ways to make jointed puppets and a puppet theater.

Vasilissa the Beautiful: A Russian Folktale. Adapted by Elizabeth Winthrop. Illustrated by Alexander Koshkin.

A beautifully illustrated retelling of a Russian fairy tale about the beautiful Vasilissa and her struggles with her wicked stepmother and stepsister. Vasilissa uses her magic doll to escape from the witch, Baba Yaga. Children love this story reminiscent of "Cinderella" and "Hansel and Gretel."

Volcano. Christopher Lampton. Illustrated with color photographs.

"I really like disaster books," commented one fourth-grader, "and the pictures in this one are great." Aberrations hold special interest for readers young and old, and this one has glossy photographs, color maps, charts, and a glossary to make it extra appealing.

Volcano! Margaret Thomas.

This well-written, nonfiction book describes some famous volcanic eruptions. Actual photographs and maps enhance the text.

Water's Way. Lisa Westberg. Illustrated by Ted Rand.

Primary children enjoy this easy reading book about the different forms that water can have, from clouds to steam to fog. They loved the pictures.

Wings. Jane Yolen. Illustrated by Dennis Molan.

Wings tells a Greek legend about Daedalus, a gifted craftsman, and his son, Icarus. The story is filled with colorful details of the legend that revolves around pride. Beautiful, sensitive watercolors.

Wonders of Science. Melvin Berger. Illustrated by G. Brian Karas.

Fascinating facts about sound, light, water, heat, and air, coupled with instructions for simple experiments that demonstrate scientific principles, make this a gold mine of information. The hands-on approach and variety of projects invite participation.

Worm's Eye View: Make Your Own Wildlife Refuge. Kipchak Johnson. Illustrated by Thompson Yardley.

How to make a wildlife refuge in your own back yard. Colorful drawings "make the book look like it is a fiction book, but the words are facts," analyzed one young reader. "That's really why kids like it."

The Wretched Stone. Chris Van Allsburg. Illustrated by the author.

Vivid illustrations depict the events in this journal written by the captain of the Rita Ann. An extraordinary, glowing rock that mysteriously turns sailors into monkeys makes this tale mesmerizing.

Older Readers

Alone in the House. Edmund Plante.

Sixteen-year-old Joanne is home alone when a mysterious stranger appears. Could he really be a vampire? One reader called it, "a blood-curdling tale you can't put down." Another warns, "It's great, but don't read it before bed."

Bully for You, Teddy Roosevelt! Jean Fritz. Illustrated by Mike Wimmer.

The twenty-sixth U.S. president, Theodore Roosevelt, was a man of many causes and passions, not wanting to waste a minute. A well-written biography about this colorful man who overcame illness to become everything from a politician to a conservationist.

Do Fishes Get Thirsty? Questions Answered by the New England Aquarium. Les Kaufman and the staff of the New England Aquarium. Illustrated with photographs.

Children loved the beautiful underwater photos in this book about the sea and its creatures. Included are the twenty-six questions that children most often ask. Some of the answers are very surprising.

Dogs Don't Tell Jokes. Louis Sachar.

Goon longs to be accepted by his peers, but his continual joking alienates everyone. The school talent show is his last hope for fame and popularity, or will he only make a fool of himself? Students comment, "It's hilarious," and "You can't put it down without a struggle."

Don't Blink Now! Capturing the Hidden World of Sea Creatures. Ann Downer. Illustrated with photographs.

Great underwater photographs of marine animals. Birth, growth, the hunt, and death are included. The reading complements the photographs with clear, precise information.

Exploring the Bismarck: The Real-Life Quest to Find Hitler's Greatest Battleship. Robert D. Ballard. Illustrated by Wesley Lowe, Ken Marshall, Jack McMaster, and Margo Stahl.

Oceanographers search the ocean floor for the battleship Bismarck, sunken fifty years ago. This story is told along with the actual events that led to the disaster. "It gave me a feeling of what the war felt like," one student said.

Finding Buck McHenry. Alfred Slote.

Eleven-year-old Jason Ross suspects the school custodian, Mack Henry, might really be the great Buck McHenry, who pitched in the old Negro leagues back when black players were excluded from the majors. This story is a mystery tale, a sports novel, and a story of how one boy's life is touched by a legend.

The Jolly Christmas Postman. Janet and Allan Ahlberg. Illustrated by the authors.

A jolly messenger, the postman, makes his rounds at Christmas with a wonderful pouch overflowing with good cheer. Letters, puzzles, and a book are tucked away into envelopes within this book.

The Jungle Book. Rudyard Kipling. Illustrated by Gregory Alexander.

"Filled with wonderful adventure stories and the paintings are exquisitely beautiful," wrote a young reader about his edition of a classic. Stories about Mowgli, the fearless man-cub, and Rikki-Tikki-Tavi, the cobra-battling mongoose, still enthrall children today.

Mama, Let's Dance. Patricia Hermes.

Mary Belle tells the story of abandoned children who survive on their own. Middle-school students were affected by this book, and asked, "How would a mother do this to her children? How could they be so self-sufficient?"

On the Tracks of Dinosaurs: A Study of Dinosaur Footprints. James O. Farlow. Illustrated by Doris Teschler.

Even students who think they know about dinosaurs are fascinated as Farlow's photographs, diagrams, and descriptions reveal how the reptiles' footprints were fossilized, how scientists study them, and what new ideas they suggest about dinosaur behavior.

Scary Stories 3: More Tales to Chill Your Bones. Collected and retold by Alvin Schwartz. Illustrated by Stephen Gammell.

By popular request, another collection of terrifying tales, including at least one true story, to thrill youngsters. The notes and sources give interesting background, and Stephen Gammell's drawings set the scene perfectly. "It might scare you," a reader warned.

The Secrets of Vesuvius: Exploring the Mysteries of an Ancient Buried City. Sara C. Bisel. Illustrated with photographs.

Part fact, part historical fiction, an archaeologist/anthropologist reconstructs the events of a small beachfront community the day before Mount Vesuvius erupts. Her story is based on excavations of bones and artifacts of the Roman town.

Ships: Sailors and the Sea. Richard Humble. Illustrated by Mark Bergin, Bill Donohoe, Nick Hewetson, Tony Townsend, Hans Wilborg-Jenssen, and Gerald Wood.

The surgeon's chest "had a mallet for knocking out the patient before operating on him." Other tidbits intrigue readers on a voyage through the history of ships. Every page has illustrations, and children like it "because it has good pictures."

The Sierra Club Book of Weatherwisdom. Vicki McVey. Illustrated by Martha Weston.

Climates and seasons, wind and rain, warm and cold fronts, atmospheric pressure, and weather predictions are discussed in this interesting book of weather. There are hands-on activities, games, and experiments. This book makes weather fun to learn.

Sluggers! Twenty-Seven of Baseball's Greatest. George Sullivan. Illustrated with photographs.

> Twenty-seven of the greatest sluggers of all time—twenty-seven outs that might constitute a pitcher's worst nightmare. Starting today with the likes of Jose Canseco and stretching back to players like Roger Connor, Sullivan brings each player to life and describes his amazing achievements.

Somewhere Between Life and Death. Lurlene McDaniel.

> The drama group's cast party was not supposed to end in tragedy. However, Amy has a horrible car accident and lies in a coma. Her parents and her sister, Erin, must find the courage to accept that Amy's life-support systems will never bring her back.

Spill! The Story of the Exxon Valdez. Terry Carr. Illustrated with photographs.

> Color photographs enhance this account of the worst oil spill in American history. As a reader noted, "It has pictures of everything it talked about." Collision, Harvest of Death, and other chapters make it a page-turner.

The Super Book of Baseball. Ron Berler. Illustrated with photographs.

> Going beyond the typical endless lists of statistics, Berler encapsulates a broad range of baseball's memorable events, teams, and players' stories. Hundreds of old and modern photographs bring to life the history of "America's favorite pastime" for young readers.

Thirteen: 13 Tales of Horror by 13 Masters of Horror. Edited by Tonya Pines.

> Thirteen horror stories from favorite authors such as Christopher Pike and R.L. Stine. Eighth-graders thought it was "chilling and suspenseful. It is a very scary book to read at night."

What Daddy Did. Neal Shusterman.

> A moving and emotional novel "about love even through bad times," wrote one student. No matter what Preston does, he always comes back to the same question: "Is it all right to kill?"

The Worst Day I Ever Had. Fred McMane and Cathrine Wolf. Photographs by Brad Hamann.

> Everyone has bad days, even heroes. This book highlights thirteen sports figures and one of the adversities they had to face in their careers. Helps to satisfy children's desire for more information about favorite athletes.

chapter sixteen
Poetry and Children

The importance of reading poetry in the classroom, as a source of literature, is emphasized in your reading and language arts methods classes. Children respond well to poetry because poetry is like music. It has a rhythm to which they can relate by marking time with their heads and hands, or by saying the words. Poetry also evokes other reactions. These reactions are sensory, imagery, and emotional response. In choosing poetry to read to children, it is important to keep in mind the ability of the child to create his or her own mental images. Remember the child who sang the hymn with the words, "Jesus, the cross-eyed bear." The child sang from his experience and the image of the cross of Jesus was not a part of his background. Start where the children are and explore a large variety of poetry. In the case of children with a deprived background, it may be necessary to help them translate it into their own experiences until they share a vivid sensory image and feel a lively emotional response.

Children have the ability to perceive other images when viewing an object that escapes us as adults. The teacher needs to capitalize on the ability so it becomes a habit throughout one's life. Take the dandelion as an example. An adult viewing a dandelion would see an obnoxious weed, difficult to destroy because of a long tap root, growing in an otherwise beautiful lawn. The view of the child is much different. He or she sees a flower blooming, ready to pick, to gather by the handful and present to mother or the teacher. Children love dandelions. Not only are they among the first flowers to appear in spring, but when they go to seed, one can blow on them and watch the seeds take flight. their stems may be used for necklaces and bracelets, and, of course, the blossom when thrust under someone's chin determines if that person likes butter. What a marvelous plant. This image of the dandelion is universal among children. What better time to build on this image than with the phrase, "Oh little soldier with the golden helmet, why are you guarding my lawn."[1], or Aileen Fischer's words, "I think they're sun prints thought."[2].

However, poetry has another dimension for the student teacher. Poetry is not only beneficial to children as literature, but to you as an adult. It helps you enter their world. A background in poetry can help you, as a teacher, increase your empathy and understanding of the children you teach. It is unfortunate that so many leave childhood behind, leaving behind the memories, the fantasy, and

---

[1]Hilda Conking, *Poems by a Little Girl*. New York: J.B. Lippincott, 1920.
[2]Aileen Fischer. Sun Prints. *Out in the Dark and the Daylight*. Harpercollins, 1980.

the excitement of being a child. For the elementary teacher, it is imperative to recapture those feelings. Randall Jarrel has said, "One of the most obvious facts about grown-ups to a child is that they have forgotten what it is like to be a child."[3]

"Know you what it is to be a child? It is to be something very different from the man . . . It is to have a spirit yet streaming from the waters of baptism; it is to believe in love . . . to believe in belief . . . it is to turn pumpkins into coaches and mice into horses!"

The question, "Know you what it is to be a child?" posed by Frances Thompson in 1908, is an important one for you to ask yourself.

Ralph Waldo Emerson once wrote, "Children are like aliens, and we treat them as such." Consider this for a moment. Think of the last interaction you observed between an adult and a child. Think of the last interaction you had with a child. Were you guilty of treating the child as an alien? Did you really understand where the child was coming from? Unfortunately, many adults find things to be a nuisance that are a pure delight to a child.

What happens in a typical classroom when the first snow of the season starts to fall? The teacher attempts to go on with the lesson. I often wonder if this is why so many classrooms have no windows, so that the excitement of the outdoors does not intrude on the reality of the classroom. How sad. The children are delighted it's snowing. The teacher may consider the snow a nuisance. The children will not learn a thing that day. If it snows all day, the buses will be late and the car may get stuck in the parking lot. Poor teacher, locked in an adult world with so little understanding of her students' excitement.

Mud is probably an even greater nuisance. "Take off those boots." "Scrape your feet." "Where did you find all that mud?" "Why didn't you stay on the blacktop?" How do children feel about mud? Polly Boyden has expressed it well:

> Mud is very nice to feel
> All squishy-squash between the toes!
> I'd rather wade in wiggly mud
> Than smell a yellow rose. [4]

Most of you may remember how you felt when a spring storm came up, catching you unprepared. You stared glumly out the window, hoping it would let up before your next class. You thought you would get soaked when you left the building. Even children must see that this is a nuisance. However, Marchette Chute wrote a poem describing an unexpected spring rain that caught a child unprepared. The child's response, "I fell into a river once but this is even better."[5]

It is important for you to be able to experience the delight and joy of the children you teach. It is important for them to know you understand how they feel.

---

[3]Randall Jarrell. *The Man Who Loved Children.* 1965. The Oxford Dictionary of Modern Quotations. New York: Oxford University Press, 1991.

[4]Polly Boyden. "Mud." *Child Life Inc.* Boston, 1930.

[5]Marchette Chute. "Spring Rain." *Rhymes About the City.* New York. Macmillan Company, 1946.

The teacher who stops the math class to share this poem when the first snow falls will share with the children in their excitement at the first snow. At that moment, the children recognize that you are sensitive to their enthusiasm. After a muddy recess, take time to share the mud poem. Give them an opportunity to discuss the niceties of mud.

> See the pretty snowflakes
> Falling from the sky
> On the walk and housetop
> Soft and thick they lie.
>
> On the window-ledges
> On the branches bare;
> Now how fast they gather
> Filling all the air. [6]

To do this you need to immerse yourself in poetry. Read it, copy it, memorize it. Build up your repertoire so you are prepared for any opportunity. You will, of course, want to read it aloud, discuss it, and use it as part of your literature program. But, most important, you want to use it to see things as children see them. Children will appreciate your increased understanding and empathy of their view of the world. They also recognize that many adults are unable to share their outlook, but what pleasure when they find one that does.

Poetry Bibliography

Arbuthnot. (1961). *Arbuthnot Anthology of Children's Literature.* Glenview: Il: Scott Foresman.

Association for Childhood Education. (1935). *Sung Under the Silver Umbrella.* Association for Childhood Education, Macmillan.

Fisher, A. (1960). *Going Barefoot.* Harper Collins.

———(1980). *Out in the Dark and the Daylight.* Harper Collins.

Hall, D. (1985). *The Oxford Book of Children's Verse in America.* New York, New York: Oxford University Press.

Heard, G. (1989). *For the Good of the Earth and Sun—Teaching Poetry.* Portsmouth, New Hampshire: Heineman.

Lear, E. (1942). *The Complete Nonsense Book.* Dodd.

---

[6]Author unknown.

McClure, A.A. (1990). *Sunrises and Songs: Reading and Writing Poetry in an Elementary Classroom*. Portsmouth, New Hampshire: Heineman.

McGinley, P. (1948). *All Around the Town*. Lippincott.

Milne, A. (1927). *Now We Are Six*. Dutton.

———(1924). *When We Were Very Young*. Dutton.

Moore, L. (1975). *See My Lovely Poison Ivy*. Anthencum.

Trapp, W. Illustrator (1973). *A Great Big Ugly Man Came Up and Tied His Horse to Me*. Little Brown and Company.

Silverstein, S. (1974). *Where the Sidewalk Ends*. Harper and Row.

———(1981). *A Light in the Attic*. Harper and Row.

Untermeyer, L. (1959). *The Golden Treasury of Poetry*. Golden Press.

chapter seventeen
Use of Magazines in the Classroom

Adult magazines have many uses in today's classroom. Old magazines are resources for art projects (cutting out pictures associated with a particular color, or pictures that begin with the same sound) and in language development to provide pictures to stimulate verbal or written stories.

Children's magazines are especially useful in providing high-interest, low-vocabulary reading material. Children turned off by books may be motivated to read magazines. This list of children's magazines provides a valuable resource for the classroom. Many will be available in your college or community library. Should you decide to subscribe, check the address; publishers tend to change addresses often.

Magazines and Periodicals for Children

This list represents magazines and periodicals available for children. However, it is not intended to be exhaustive. It should serve as a basic resource to which new magazines may be added as they become available.

Boy's Life

Boy Scouts of America, published monthly, 1325 Walnut Hill Lane, P.O. Box 152079, Irving, Texas 75015. Fiction and non-fiction; much information on outdoor life.

Chickadee

Published ten times, P.O. Box 11314, Des Moines, Iowa 50304. Naturalist magazine for children up to nine years.

Child's Life

Ben Franklin Society, published monthly, bi-monthly in the summer, P.O. Box 7133, Red Oak, Iowa 51591. Variety of stories, art, and science for ages 9-11.

Children's Playmate

> Published monthly, except summer, P.O. Box 7133, Red Oak, Iowa 51591. Stories, poetry, and riddles for ages 6-8.

Cobblestone

> Published monthly, except July and August, Cobblestone Publishing, 7 School Street, Peterborough, New Hampshire 03458. History magazine for young people.

3-2-1 Contact

> Published monthly, except February and August, P.O. Box 53051, Boulder, Colorado. Science and technology articles of interest to ages 8-14.

Crickett

> Published monthly, Box 387, Mt. Morris, Illinois 61054. Short stories, poems, contest, and puzzles for ages 8-14.

Ebony, Jr.

> Published monthly, Johnson Publishing Company, 820 S. Michigan Avenue, Chicago, Illinois 60605. Stories, articles, and games in the life of blacks, accepts children's original works, ages K-6.

Fun Zone

> Published monthly, except bi-monthly in June and July, Highlights for Children, 2300 West 5th, P.O. Box 269, Columbus, Ohio. Stories, games, puzzles, especially hidden pictures.

Highlights for Children

> Published monthly, except bi-monthly in July and August, Department C.A., P.O. Box 182051, Columbus, Ohio 43218. Includes fun with word problems, stories, and crafts.

Humpty-Dumpty

> Published monthly, Parents Magazine, P.O. Box 7133, Red Oak, Iowa 51591. Activities for young children, easy to read stories, poetry, songs, science, and nature for ages 4-6.

International Wildlife

> Published monthly, National Wildlife Federation, 8925 Leesburg Pike, Vienna, Virginia 22182. Excellent pictures and articles on nature, ecology, high reading level.

Jack and Jill

> Published monthly, Benjamin Franklin Society, P.O. Box 7133, Red Oak, Iowa 51591. Stories span several levels of reading ability, accepts original work by children.

Kid City

> Formerly Electric Company, published monthly, except February and August, P.O. Box 53349, Boulder, Colorado 80322. For graduates of Sesame Street, ages 6-10.

Kids Discover

> Published ten times a year, P.O. Box 554206, Boulder, Colorado 80323. Each issue explores one topic, kids discover oceans, etc., for ages 8-14.

Model Airplane News

> Published monthly, Air Age, Inc., 251 Danburg Road, Wilton, Connecticut 06897. For youngsters interested in model building.

National Geographic World

> Published monthly, P.O. Box 98006, Washington, D.C. 20090. Written for children from society materials, also games and activities.

Odyssey

> Published ten times a year, 7 School Street, Peterborough, New Hampshire 03458. Space exploration and astronomy for young people.

Owl, the Discovery Magazine for Kids

> Published monthly, except July and August, Young Naturalist Foundation, 255 Great Arrow Avenue, Buffalo, New York 14207. Articles on nature, conservation for ages 7-14.

Ranger Rick

> Published monthly, National Wildlife Foundation, 8925 Leesburg Pike, Vienna, Virginia 22184. Nature magazine with excellent articles, projects, good color photography for ages 5-12.

Sesame Street

> Published monthly, except February and August, P.O. Box 52000, Boulder, Colorado 80321. Comes with a guide, lots of pictures, few words, instruction in English and Spanish, ages 2-6.

Sports Illustrated for Kids

> Published monthly, Time Magazine, P.O. Box 830609, Birmingham, Alabama 35283. Articles on sports and participants written for kids.

Super Science

Eight monthly issues, Scholastic Magazine, P.O. Box 3710, Jefferson City, Missouri 65102. Level I for grades 1-3, Level II for grades 4-6, articles and activities of science in action.

Zillions

Published bi-monthly, Consumers Reports/Zillions Classroom Programs, P.O. Box 3760, Department 8071, Jefferson City, Missouri 65102. On the format of Consumer's Guide for adults, rates movies, music, and items kids would purchase, ages 7-14.

chapter eighteen
Orientation to the First Clinical Experience Classroom

Upon arrival at your assigned school you will, in most cases, be met by the principal. He or she will probably talk with you, give you an initial introduction to the school, and take you on a tour of the building. Then you will be taken to your assigned classroom where you will meet your cooperating teacher, in some cases for the first time.

The school day is about to begin and there may be many things you would like to know and ask. Then your cooperating teacher shows you where to hang up your coat, gives you a corner to put your belongings, and invites you to welcome the children as they arrive. Next, he or she hands you a folder to browse through at your convenience that morning, and says you will have a chance to talk together when the class goes to music later that morning.

You can begin to feel a bit more relaxed. It is good to have a little time to reflect on the message from the principal, and to go over in your mind the brief tour of the building. At last, you have met your cooperating teacher and been warmly welcomed. Now you are eager to see what the folder has to offer.

The folder contains basic classroom information, emergency and first-aid procedures, a copy of the daily schedule minus lesson plans, a picture roster of the class, a list of students leaving the room for other assignments, a list of reading and math groups, and a diagram of the room showing location of materials and equipment. The cooperating teacher created this folder to have in his or her file at all times in the event of an unexpected absence. Everything contained in the folder is essential information used daily by the classroom teacher. By placing it all together, it is readily available to a substitute or other professional educators working in the classroom. By now, you are aware of how much necessary information, scheduling, and organization goes into the teacher's job.

Classroom Information

Classroom teacher: _____ Home phone: _____

Helping teacher (aide or other): _____

Room location: _____

Helpful students (ones you could rely on to give accurate information in your absence): _____

_____

_____

_____

A substitute teacher should assume any extra duties the regular teacher has scheduled for the day. The clinical students and/or student teachers will participate in any extra duties with the regular teacher present.

Method for lunch count and attendance: _____

_____

_____

_____

Location of adult washrooms: _____

_____

_____

Routine for beginning and ending the day (pledge, etc.) _____

_____

_____

_____

Tardy students—What to do about: _____

_____

_____

Rules for students leaving classroom (bathroom, learning center, library, patrol duty, lunchroom duty, etc.): _____

_____

Where keys are located: _____

_____

Who runs AV equipment: _____

_____

_____

Where AV equipment is located: _____

_____

_____

Location and use of ditto/thermofax machines: _____

_____

_____

Where class supplies are located (paper and supply forms for lunch count and attendance, chalk, etc.): _____

_____

_____

_____

Classroom rules: _____

_____

_____

This would include a list of the employed procedures for daily routines:

1. What children are expected to do as they arrive each morning.
2. Lunch money and count/pledge.
3. Bathroom routine.
4. Getting drinks: what the teacher allows.
5. Recess: how to line up, proper exit, any other rules.
6. Lunch: how to line up, hot or cold line up first, etc.
7. How the children have been taught to get materials (workbook, sharpen pencils, etc.) ready each day.
8. Method of collecting and/or passing out work.
9. How the teacher goes about having children make corrections in their work.
10. Grading: process to follow.
11. Sending work home: some do this daily, others have folders to send home once each week.
12. Policy for use of independent activities: classroom library, learning stations, educational games, etc.
13. Any other classroom rules.

Each teacher has his or her own style that fits the system, while filling his or her needs and those of the children. As a student teacher or substitute, it is important to be as consistent as possible by maintaining the basic normal routines. The children become patterned in these procedures, and to have "visitors" pay heed to them adds to their sense of comfort and security.

Emergency and First-Aid Procedures

Fire drill—List rules, list evacuation directions, and location: _____

_____

_____

_____

Tornado drill—List rules, list evacuation direction and location: _____

_____

_____

_____

_____

Injured students—Explain correct procedures: _____

_____

_____

_____

Ill Students—Explain correct procedures: _____

_____

_____

_____

List of students with special health concerns:

Name_____ Diabetic _____ need to _____

Name_____ Epileptic _____ need to _____

Name_____ Vision _____ seat near board _____

Name_____ Hearing _____ left ear loss _____

Name_____ Bladder weakness _____ 2-3 trips each a.m. _____

2-3 trips each p.m. _____

Example: Daily Class Schedule

Time	Monday	Tuesday	Wednesday	Thursday	Friday
8:50-9:00	PLEDGE, ATTENDANCE, LUNCH COUNT, OTHER BUSINESS				
	Write in time estimates and subjects taught on various days—language arts, math, social studies, science, health.				
10:30-10:45	RECESS				
11:40-12:10	LUNCH				

In remaining spaces you would write in any other out of classroom schedules—art, music, physical education, library, computer, learning center.

| 3:00 | DISMISSAL | | | | |

Students Leaving the Room

This would include children who go to speech, counseling, learning disabilities classroom, reading class, etc.

Student	Purpose	Day	Leave	Return

_____

_____

_____

_____

_____

_____

_____

_____

_____

_____

What to do When the Lesson Plan Runs Out

Activities: _____

_____

_____

_____

_____

_____

Location of ditto papers, educational games, etc.: _____

_____

_____

_____

_____

_____

Location of teacher manuals and guides (and codes used in plan book).
Example: SF (Scott Foresman):

_____

_____

_____

_____

_____

Seating Chart

There are several ways to handle seating arrangements. With ever-changing desk arrangements, and switching the children from one location to another, this is a difficult process to keep updated.

Large name tags could be contained in this folder, to be stood on each child's desk as needed.

Some teachers have name tags taped to the front side of each child's desk. This is fine until you choose to place the desks together in table fashion, thus hiding the names. Others elect to have children equipped with tags in their desks.

Another personal touch would be to make a chart with the picture and name of each child. Pictures are taken in most schools at the beginning of the school year, and each teacher gets copies of each child in his or her class.

chapter nineteen
Four Minutes to Go!
Now What?

One of the dilemmas student teachers and beginning teachers face is what to do when they have unplanned time. This may occur when the lesson is too short, when the students have a few spare minutes before going to an assembly, or filing in for lunch, or when waiting for another teacher. It happens to all teachers at one time or another. The difference is the more experienced teacher will have some ideas to constructively use the time.

Here are some helpful suggestions. They have not been designated primary or intermediate; you should make that decision yourself. Simon Says, for example, is intended for K-1. On the other hand, the game Twenty Questions could be adapted to any elementary level, depending on the object to identify. Upper-grade students find it a good activity in which they may play the role of leader.

Simon Says

The teacher may begin the game and later choose a student to take the lead. It is a good choice of a game to use when students are getting restless and need to do some moving. The game is also good for increasing listening skills. The rules are that students only respond to the directions when they are preceded by the words, "Simon says." For example: "Simon says, stand up. Simon says, turn around. Simon says, shake your hands. Sit down." Those who sat down would be out, because the direction was not preceded by Simon says.

Picture This

This is a great way to have fun with the spelling list. Divide the class into two teams (often it is a good idea to pick teams by choosing one half of the room to compete against the other). One student from team A is picked to be the drawer. A student from team B is the guesser. The teacher shows the drawer the word. He draws it on the board, without using any words or numbers. The guesser attempts to guess the word. Once the guesser knows the word, he or she must write it on the board using correct spelling. Teams get a point for each word guessed and spelled correctly.

Tic-Tac-Toe

A number grid is placed on the board. The student must answer a question corresponding with the number he or she chooses. Correct answers get an X or an O depending on where it is on the grid. The questions may come from any area of the curriculum. While it makes an excellent review game, it may also be used with current topics of the day. This game may also be played as a team.

Password

Clues to assist students trying to guess the word are printed on index cards. They may be compiled by the students who have researched the subject to come up with clues, ranging from more difficult to easy. For example, if the word to be guessed is Illinois, some of the clues might be: it is the Prairie State, it produces corn and soybeans, it is sometimes called the Land of Lincoln, etc. Points are decided by the number of guesses required.

The Name Game

This game is useful for reviewing information about story characters, historical figures, or current newsmakers. One student starts the game. The teacher tapes a character's name to the student's back without him or her seeing it. The student shows the rest of the class his or her back, then tries to figure out the person's identity by asking questions. He or she may only ask questions that may be answered with a "yes" or "no." For example: "Am I a leader of a country?" The student has ten questions to determine the secret identity.

Pass the Globe

The students sit in a circle and the teacher holds out the globe. The teacher calls the name of a student and rolls the globe to that student. The teacher asks the question, "Can you find both North and South America on the globe?" If the student answers correctly, he or she rolls the globe to another student and gets to ask the question.

Eagle Feathers

Make a large headband of sturdy cardboard. Attach twenty or thirty feathers to it with paper clips (this way the activities may be easily changed). The student selects a feather and performs the task that it is written on it. For example: Add three numbers, recite the months of the year, or write five short vowel words.

Pantomimes

Give the student a card with an activity on it. He or she performs it, and the class tries to guess what the student is doing. Some ideas: making a bed, putting a puzzle together, or eating spaghetti.

Open-Ended Phrases

Give the selected student an open-ended phrase such as: "Something that makes me feel good is," "If I could give everyone in the world something, it would be," etc. That student shares his or her ideas with the class and then chooses the next participant.

Participating Stories

Tell the class you are going to read them a story, but they are going to help. You may then assign parts either to an individual or to a group of students. You could also create your own story that has repetitive phrases such as The Three Little Pigs, where the children repeat "Little pig, little pig, let me come in," and "Not by the hair of my chinney chin chin."

The Gigantic Giant that Hated Birds

Review with your class the characters and the sounds they make. Whenever a character is mentioned, have the children say the special sound.

The Gigantic Giant	Grrr (look like a giant)
Birds	Peep, peep, whistle (flap arms)
Magic sword	Puff, swish, (wave sword)
Elegant eagle	Squawk (flap arms)
Fabulous unicorn	Cup hands for horn (a-woo), gallop with hands on legs

The story goes like this: Once upon a time there lived a gigantic giant that hated birds. Now, this giant lived on top of a high hill overlooking the forest. Every morning when the birds were eating breakfast, the gigantic giant would come out with his magic sword and bat the birds into the next country. The gigantic giant would jump up and down laughing so hard the whole forest would shake and the birds would lose their breakfast.

One morning the gigantic giant brought out his magic sword and batted Elegant Eagle into the next country. The gigantic giant jumped up and down laughing so hard that all the animals for miles around got sick and shook up. The Fabulous Unicorn did not like getting shook up. The Fabulous Unicorn had the body and head of a horse (gallop with hands), the tail of a lion (roar), and a single horn (a-woo) in the middle of his forehead.

But what could a Fabulous Unicorn, an Elegant Eagle and a flock of birds do to stop a gigantic giant and his magic sword that batted birds into the next country? Well, it was decided that the birds and Elegant Eagle would all flock together and weave a net from feathers to capture the gigantic giant that hated birds. The Fabulous Unicorn stuffed the feather net into his horn. The next morning, the gigantic giant brought out his magic sword expecting to bat birds into the next country. Instead, the Fabulous Unicorn galloped up and blew the feather net out of his horn and all over the gigantic giant that hated birds. Elegant Eagle rushed up and grabbed the magic sword. All of a sudden, (puff, boom), the gigantic giant turned into a pipsqueak giant (roar in high pitched voice) and ran away. The birds, Elegant Eagle, and the Fabulous Unicorn buried the magic sword so no one could use it again because who really likes to be batted into the next country and lose their breakfast?

Dictionary Skills

To practice dictionary skills, the teacher writes a letter and a topic on the board. For example: B—a kind of bird. The students think of the word and locate it in the dictionary. The student will read the meaning when they find it. Words might include, bluebird, blackbird, etc.

Riddle Me This

Keep a good supply of riddles at your desk. Index cards are a good way to organize them so you can keep track of the ones you have already used. A good source of riddles may be found in the children's magazine, *Highlights,* and in *The Teacher's Almanack.* [1]

---

[1] *The Teacher's Almanack.* The Center for Applied Research in Education Inc., West Nyack, New York, 1980.

Children of all ages respond well to riddles, partly because they are eager to try them on someone else.

Around the World

This is a game that may be played with any skill you are working on, arithmetic facts, vocabulary recognition, etc. Two children compete to see who can get the sum of two numbers faster, after the teacher shows the flashcard. The first two children stand up to compete. The winner then stands behind (or next to the third child) and waits to see the next flashcard. The game continues in this way around the class. The winner is the one who defeats all the others or has gone "Around the World."

Twenty Questions

This is an excellent activity for reinforcing listening skills. The game requires a box (a shoe box will do nicely). The teacher or a student places an object in the box. The students then have to guess its identity. Questions to gain information must be phrased so they receive a "yes" or "no" answer. They may ask, "Is it red?" They may not ask, "What color is it?" The leader tallies the "no" responses on the board. If twenty have been recorded without the student guessing what is in the box, the leader is the winner.

Huckle Buckle Beanstalk

Have a small object not typically found in a classroom—like a small spool of thread, a miniature souvenir spoon, or a skeleton key. With all eyes closed, one person hides the object by putting it in a spot where it is partially hidden from view. The children move about the room with both hands behind their backs, using only their eyes. When a student sees the object, he or she returns to the seat and calls out huckle-buckle-beanstalk. This way, no one knows where the individual spotted the object, and the others can go on looking until everyone has found it. The first one to find the object is the next one to hide it. This is a good game for increasing observation skills and learning to explore beyond normal eye level (both high and low).

I'm Thinking of Something

The leader says, "I'm thinking of something in this room that begins with the letter C." Children are called on to give their answers—chalk, crayons, Cathy, chalkboard, chair, carpet, clock, ceiling, until the correct answer is given. The child with the correct answer is the next leader. When appropriate, children can be asked to explain the beginning sound: C sounds like K, C sounds like S, or to identify the vowel sound found in their answer.

These activities make good use of short periods of time and help maintain group control while having some relaxing fun moments. Some of these give practice in basic skills, some encourage physical activity, some focus on use of observation or listening strengths, and most give students a chance to be the leader.

Have enough "time fillers" to use in appropriate situations, and to provide variety and interest for your class.

chapter twenty
Field Trip Ideas

It is possible that as a first clinical experience student you may go on a field trip with your class. This is a good time to become aware of the potential learning value that is available to children through quality field trips. Take an overview of the area to which you are assigned and see what might be available learning experiences. Later, in your student-teaching semester, you may have a chance to incorporate a field trip into your planned activities.

Use this time to ask questions about field trip procedure, permission slips, legal transportation requirements (are parent drivers allowed?), payment of admission fees for less-able families, student-chaperon ratios, and pre- and post-teaching responsibilities. These may vary in school districts, but it will begin to give you a feel for the process.

When you are on your own as a teacher, you will want to organize information on possible educational ventures in your new area. The chamber of commerce, local libraries and newspapers, and the teaching staff can get you started. If you are near a large city, you have yet another arena to research. Some local field trips that could have merit would be:

airport	greenhouse
police station	newspaper
fire station	library
post office	pumpkin farm
courthouse	hospital
natural area or forest preserve	radio station
local factories, if appropriate	bank
farm	train station
water treatment plant	retirement home
apple orchard	recycling plant

A university, where there are many cultural exhibits, shows, and concerts, is also a potential field trip site.

In urban areas consider:

museums	zoo
science centers	animal parks
hands-on discovery centers	center for health education
aquariums	environmental center
botanic garden	conservation areas

Field trips, while having educational merit when used well, can be expensive and, therefore, are often limited. Consider bringing the community to your classroom. Invite interesting individuals to the classroom who can present their particular skills, careers, or travel experiences.

You need to balance your academic curriculum and your visitors and field trips to create constructive and vital learning experiences. Some of these ideas might help you to get started.

chapter twenty-one
Teacher Resources

There are a vast number of resources available for teachers. An exciting array of magazines with ideas for bulletin boards, art projects, individual and unit lesson plans, and tips for teachers on discipline, curriculum, ways to deal with parents, etc., are available along with the usual subject matter journals. For the student or beginning teacher, the problem is not availability, but making a choice of which publication would best serve his or her needs. This list of magazines is designed to help you make that decision. Should you decide to order one of these publications, it would be advisable to make a phone call to be sure the address is still current.

Teacher Magazines

Instructor, Incorporating Teacher
The Instructor
P.O. Box 53896
Boulder, Colorado 80322

This magazine should be in your university library. Many schools also have a copy available. However, if you really want to keep abreast of current issues in education, and have the most recent ideas to use in the classroom, it is a good choice for your own library. In addition to a monthly planner, bulletin board, art ideas, poetry, and science projects, the magazine also includes articles on curriculum and other informative subjects.

Schooldays (Primary: 800-333-3580)
Classmates (Secondary: 800-421-5565)
P.O. Box 2853
Torrance, California 90509

These magazines are published four times a year and are filled with practical ideas for elementary teachers. Both issues include reproducible units, science lessons, art ideas, bulletin boards, and successful teaching techniques.

Teaching K-8
P.O. Box 512
Farmingdale, New York 11737
800-678-8793

Along with monthly articles on curriculum issues, regular features include education newswatch, teaching math, teaching science, professional growth, the teaching K-8 shopper, what is new in professional teaching aids, and recommended books for the month.

Lollipops, Magazine for Preschool and Early Childhood Education
Good Apple Publishers
P.O. Box 299
Carthage, Illinois 62321
217-357-3981

An excellent magazine for early childhood, kindergarten and first grade. The publication includes timely teaching tips, bulletin boards, cut-and-paste activities, craft projects, songs, fingerplays, game boards, and a monthly calendar.

Oasis (5-9)
Good Apple Publication
P.O. Box 299
Carthage, Illinois 62321
217-357-3981

A resource for the middle-school teacher, this publication is also useful in the upper elementary grades. Five issues per school year include reproducible pages, biographies, calendars, book reviews, composition boards, environmental units, and tips to teachers from teachers.

Challenge, A Magazine for Reaching and Teaching the Gifted Child
Good Apple Publication
P.O. Box 299
Carthage, Ilinois 62321
217-357-3981

This magazine provides ready-to-use creative and critical thinking reproducible activities, and articles from leaders in gifted children.

The following publications have a newspaper format.

The Good Apple Newspaper (2-8)
A Good Apple Publication
P.O. Box 299
Carthage, Ilinois 62321
217-357-3481

Copycat
P.O. Box 081546
Racine, Wisconsin 53408
414-634-0146

These newspapers are similar in approach. Both contain creative, easy-to-use ideas for every area of the curriculum. There are many seasonal activities, arts and crafts, bulletin boards, and unique units of study.

Professional Journals

The following section includes journals that are essential to keep up with the latest research and ideas in the respective fields. Most of these are available in your university library. Time spent reading the latest issues will keep you current on educational issues.

The Reading Teacher
Journal of the International Reading Association
800 Barksdale Road
P.O. Box 8139
Newark, Delaware 19714

This publication includes sections on evaluation and recommended use of children's books, links literary research with instructional practice, includes practical ideas for classroom use, and recommends books for teachers to read. Included in the fall issues is a complete list of favorite books chosen by students and teachers .

The Arithmetic Teacher
NCTM Dept. M
1906 Association Drive
Reston, Virginia 22091

The publication includes materials to use with K-8. A section on Calendar Mathematics gives weekly activities, further divided into grade-level projects. Also included are articles on putting research into practice, math and technology, reviews of computer materials, and new books on mathematics for children and teachers.

Science and Children, A Journal Devoted to Pre-school Through Middle School Science Teaching
National Science Teachers Association
1742 Connecticut Avenue N.W.
Washington, D.C. 20009

The journal includes recommended books and resources for teachers, ideas for complete science units, early childhood science activities, and important research in science education.

School Supply Stores *

Alabama
Albertville: Kaylor's School and Office Supply
Birmingham: Burrow School Supply; The Re-Print Corp.
Huntsville: Schoolcraft

Alaska
Anchorage: Learning Works
Fairbanks: Schoolhouse Express

Arizona
Glendale: The Teaching Center
Tucson: Jonathan's Educational Resources; Teaching Tools Company
Phoenix: Teaching Tools Company
Tempe: Teaching Tools Company
Mesa: Teaching Tools Company

Arkansas
Sherwood: A+ Teaching Supplies

California
Bakersfield: Learning Stop
Buena Park: Teachers Supplies
Carson: Lakeshore Curriculum
Chico: Creative Apple
Chula Vista: Educational Supplies Plus
Citrus Heights: The Report Card
Concord: Warren's Educational Supplies
Covina: Warren's Educational Supplies
Culver City: Social Studies School Service
Fresno: G & W School Supply
Goleta: Bennett's Educational Materials
Long Beach: Teacher Supplies of Long Beach
Los Angeles: Social Service Company
Northridge: Syl-bern's Educational Station
Oakland: Oakland Parent Teacher Store
Oceanside: Learning Capital
Palo Alto: Dale Seymour Publications
Petaluma: HBJ Beckley-Cardy Inc.
Pomona: CM School Supply
Rosemead: Warren's Educational Supplies
Sacramento: Toys That Teach; Teacher's Exchange
San Carlos: Morrison School Supply
San Diego: Parent Store; Sea World
San Jose: Teachers Supply House; Teacher's Helper
San Ramon: Golden Apple

Santa Rosa:	Skool Daze Teacher's Supplies
Solana Beach:	Creative Teaching Supplies
Thousand Oaks:	New Horizons
Venture:	Bennett's Educational Materials

Colorado

| Arvada: | Teacher's Helper Colorado Springs. |
| Colorado Springs: | Teacher's Pet |

Connecticut

Danbury:	Teacher-Parent Store
Hartford:	HP Kopplemann Inc.
South Norwalk:	Hammett's Teacher's Store

District of Columbia

| Washington: | Crown Educational and Teaching Aids; Learning Ideas; National Science Teachers Association |

Florida

Brandon:	Teacher's Helper Inc.
Coral Springs:	Hammett's Learning World
Fort Myers:	School Stuff
Greenwood Acres:	Teach of Palm Beach
Hialeah:	Drago School Equipment
Jacksonville:	All-Florida Supply
Miami:	Get Smart
Orlando:	Central Florida School
Pensacola:	Hammett's Learning World
Plantation:	ABC Educational Supplies

Georgia

Augusta:	School Day Supply Company
Duluth:	ABC School Supply
Forest Park:	Key's Learning World
Macon:	Georgia School Supply
Tucker:	School Tools & Office Pals

Hawaii

| Aiea: | Hands On |
| Honolulu: | Film Services of Hawaii |

Idaho

| Boise: | Idaho Book and School Supply |

Illinois

Arlington Heights:	Hammett's Learning World
Belleville:	Teacher's Aid
Bloomingdale:	Educational Aids
Buffalo Grove:	Educational Aids
Chicago:	Gray's Distributing Company

Country Club Hills:	Teacher's Storehouse
Joliet:	The Chalkboard
Oak Park:	Universal Four
Orlando Park:	Schoolworks
Rockford:	The 3Rs Learning Materials Center
Schaumburg:	Educational Aids Inc.; HBJ Beckley-Cardy Inc.
Springfield:	The School Bag
Tinley Park:	Teacher's Corner
West Chicago:	HBJ Beckley-Cardy Inc.

Indiana

Clarksville:	Kentucky School Service
Fort Wayne:	United Supply Company; Kelso Inc.
Indianapolis:	Seeds for Knowledge; Parent/Teacher Education World; The Learning Depot
Lafayette:	Teacher's Delight
Muncie:	Kelso Inc.
Schererville:	School Stuff Inc.
South Bend:	Creative Teaching

Iowa

Bettendorf:	Wise Owl Inc.
Cedar Falls:	J.S. Latta & Sons; Latta's West
Cedar Rapids:	Metropolitan Supply Company
Council Bluffs:	Learning Explorations
Dubuque:	Wise Owl Inc.
West Des Moines:	The Learning Post

Kansas

Dodge City:	Superior School Products
Leawood:	U.S. Toy Company Inc.
Overland Park:	The Supply Closet
Pittsburgh:	Bowlus School Supply Company
Salina:	School Specialty Supply
Shawnee:	The Teacher's Store
Topeka:	School Specialty Supply
Wichita:	Superior School Supplies Inc.
Bowling Green:	Southern School Supply Inc.
Covington:	J.R. Green Company
Elizabeth Town:	Kentucky School Service; Thoroughbred Publisher
Lexington:	Educator's Delight
Louisville:	Central School Supply; Kentucky School Service

Louisiana

Baton Rouge:	School Aids
Bossier City:	The Paper Shack

Gretna:	Educator Educational Supplies
Lafayette:	J & R Educational Supplies
Monroe:	The Teacher's Mart Inc.

Maine

Augusta:	The Painted Horse

Maryland

Baltimore:	Hammett's Teacher Store; School and Preschool
Columbia:	Chaselle Inc.
Gaithersburg:	Hammett's Learning World

Massachusetts

Braintree:	Hammett's Learning World; J.L. Hammett Co.
Framington:	Hammett's Teacher's Store
Holyoke:	Hammett's Teacher's Store
Springfield:	New England School Supply

Michigan

Detroit:	Multi-Media Education
Grand Rapids:	Grow and Learn; mpi The Teacher's Store
Holland:	Apple Tree Educational Supplies
Lansing:	mpi The Teacher's Store
Livonia:	mpi The Teacher's Store
Sterling Heights:	mpi The Teacher's Store; The Learning Tree

Minnesota

Arden Hills:	St. Paul Book and Stationary
Brooklyn Center:	St. Paul Book and Stationary
Burnsville:	Classroom Connections; St. Paul Book and Stationary
Duluth:	Beckley-Cardy Company
Eden Praries:	St. Paul Book and Stationary
Minneapolis:	St. Paul Book and Stationary
Minnetonka:	St. Paul Book and Stationary
Signal Hills:	St. Paul Book and Stationary
St. Cloud:	The Bookworm

Mississippi

Jackson:	Martin School Equipment Company; Missco Corporation

Missouri

Grandview:	U.S. Toy Company
Kansas City:	The Teacher's Store
Springfield:	IPA Educational Supply
St. Louis:	Bradburn School Supply; The Teacher's Store
Washington:	Paperbacks for Educators

Montana
    Great Falls: Northern School Supply
    Missoula: Great Northern Book Company

Nebraska
    Lincoln: Stephenson's School Supply
    Omaha: Stephenson's School Supply

Nevada
    Las Vegas: Learning is Fun
    Reno: Parent-Teacher Aids

New Jersey
    Burlington: Hammett's Teacher's Store
    Hawthorne: A W Peller & Associates Inc.
    Middletown: Hammett's Teacher's Store
    Morristown: The Teaching Room
    Mt. Laurel: HBJ Beckley-Cardy Inc.
    Pennsauken: Roberts Bros. Inc.
    Phillipsburg: Hammett's Teacher's Store
    Tom's River: Hammett's Teacher's Store
    Union: J Hammett
    Verona: Hammett's Learning World
    Woodbridge: Hammett's Teacher's Store

New Mexico
    Albuquerque: Allied School & Office Products

New York
    Amityville: L L Weans & Company
    Brooklyn: Barclay School Supplies
    Buffalo: Laurence P Paul Teacher's Pet Inc.;
                       United Educational Services
    Fishkill: Hammett's Teacher's Stores
    Lyons: J. L. Hammett Company
    Medford: Island School and Art Supplies District
    Poughkeepsie: Golden Apple
    Queens Village: Nick Breglio Inc.
    Rochester: Teacher's World
    Spring Valley: A+ Discount Distributors
    White Plains: The Teacher's Room

North Carolina
    Asheville: Morgan Brothers School Supplies
    Atlantic Beach: Teacher's Pet
    Belmont: School Specialities Company
    Charlotte: Hammett's Learning World
    Greensboro: Education Center; Edu-Play
    Kernersville: I E S S Inc.

Mooresville: Hammett's Learning World
Pollocksville: Bender & Sons School Supply
Salisbury: Creative Teaching Aids

North Dakota
Fargo: Northern School Supply Company

Ohio
Akron: Creative Curriculum
Beaver Creek: Creative Learning Consultants
Cleveland: Holcumb's Educational Materials
Columbus: Holcumb's Educational Materials
Dayton: Holcumb's Educational Materials;
                     F & S Enterprises
Mansfield: Opportunities for Learning;
                     Frey Scientific Company
Maple Heights: Holcumb's Educational Materials
N. Olmstead: Holcumb's Educational Materials
Reynoldsburg: Teacher's Helper East
Trotwood: The Learning Ladder

Oklahoma
Ada: Thompson Book and Supply Company
Durant: Thompson Book and Supply Company
Edmond: Thompson Book and Supply Company
Oklahoma City: Thompson Book and Supply Company;
                     Classroom Connections; Hoover Bros. Inc.
Tulsa: The Apple Tree Inc.

Oregon
Beaverton: Learning World
Eugene: School Daze
Portland: Learning Palace; Learning World

Pennsylvania
Bristol: Barclay School Supply
Clearfield: Kurtz Brothers Inc.
Grove City: Schooldays Supply Shop
Harrisburg: Edu-Care Services Inc.
Lancaster: Education Station Inc.
Philadelphia: Center for Applied Psychology;
                     Charles J. Becker and Bros.
Roslyn: Paine Learning Aids Center of Philadelphia

South Carolina
Charleston: Hammett's Learning World
Columbia: Educational Wonderland;
                     Hammett's Teacher's Store
Greenville: Hammett's Learning World
Myrtle Beach: Teacher's Touch Inc.

South Dakota
      Sioux Falls: Dakota News; Teacher's Helper

Tennessee
      Bristol: Kentucky School Service
      Chattanooga: P & S Paper and School Supply
      Knoxville: P & S Paper and School Supply
      Madison: P & S Paper and School Supply
      Maryville: National School Products
      Nashville: Acme School Supply Company

Texas
      Arlington: Education
      Austin: Good Books
      Beaumont: Manning's School Supply
      Carrollton: Hoover Brothers Inc.
      Conroe: The Schoolhouse Store
      Dallas: Hoover Brothers Inc.
      El Paso: Eraser Dust
      Fort Worth: Murray Teaching Aids
      Houston: Southwest Teacher Supply
      Hurst: Teacher's Tools
      Lubbock: Sentinel Book Store Inc.
      Lufkin: HBJ Beckeley-Cardy Inc.
      McAllen: Rio Grande Book Company
      Mesquite: Hoover Brothers Inc.
      Midland: Creative Schoolhouse
      N. Richland Hills: Hoover Brothers Inc.
      Pasadena: WB Cole Supply
      San Antonio: ECS Learning Systems Inc.
      Temple: Hoover Brothers Inc.

Utah
      Murray: U I Investor Inc.
      Ogden: Alphabet Station
      Orem: Alphabet Station
      Salt Lake City: Alphabet Station; Thought Provokers

Virginia
      Glenallen: Hammett's Teacher's Store
      Lynchburg: J. L. Hammett
      Norfolk: Hammett's Teacher's Store
      Oakton: Hammett's Teacher's Store
      Richmond: Hammett's Teacher's Store; Teach 'N Things
      Springfield: Hammett's Teacher's Store
      Sterling: Schoolworks
      Virginia Beach: The Teacher's Aide Inc.

Washington
  Bellevue: Academic Aids Inc.; Learning World Inc.
  Federal Way: Learning World Inc.
  Kent: Academic Supplies
  Lynnwood: Learning World Inc.
  Olympia: School Daze
  Seattle: University Book Store; Learning World Inc.
  Spokane: Learning World Inc.

West Virginia
  Huntington: Education Emporium;
                               Latta Divison of Okhai-Moyer

Wisconsin
  Appleton: Learning Shop; Valley School Suppliers
  Fort Atkinson: The Highsmith Company; NASCO
  Green Bay: The SchoolHouse
  Madison: Madison School Supply Company; Demco
  Stevens Point: Play 'N Learn Educational Aids
  West Allis: Teacher's Pet Inc.

* 1991 *listing; used with permission from Good Apple Publishers.*

glossary

Competitive Learning: Student performance is judged against the average performance of all students.

Cooperating Teacher: The teacher working with the children in the classroom to which the clinical student is assigned.

Cooperative Learning: Children work together in small, often heterogeneous groups, in which each member of the group has a defined role, and each member shares in the responsibility for the learning of everyone in the group.

Direct Lesson: Teacher tells the concept to be learned and leads the students through the appropriate activities.

First Clinical Student: A sophomore, junior, senior, or graduate student who is in his or her first formal experience of working with children in a classroom. The clinical experience requires two full days of workshop followed by six full days in the classroom.

Inductive Lesson: Begins with exploratory activities and leads students to discover the concept.

Pupil Personnel Services: A group of specialists working to provide professional services for students identified as being in need of a specific service beyond the classroom setting. The student is first identified as having a need for an extended service, it is communicated to the parents who in turn give their permission for any appropriate testing that may be required to positively identify the needs, and then it is brought before the PPS (Pupil Personnel Services) Team for appropriate review and assignment of services. This could include speech needs, health needs, learning disabilities, behavior disorders, social and psychological needs. Therefore, the team usually consists of the school district psychologist, the principal, social worker, and the special education and learning disabilities teachers assigned to that particular building. The team would further include the teacher of the child potentially in need of services. The parents would be invited to share in the final meeting that would report test findings and recommendations for giving support to their child's specific needs within the educational setting.

Second Clinical Student: A second clinical student engaged in his or her second semester of supervised teaching and related activities. This experience builds upon the first clincal experience and includes more in-depth approaches in the areas covered in this text. Students have campus class time directed to language arts, social studies, math, science, and an outdoor education experience. They spend three full weeks in a regular elementary classroom.

Student Teacher: Having successfully completed both the first and second clinical experiences, the student then devotes a full semester to student teaching in a regular elementary classroom under the guidance of the university supervisor and the classroom (cooperating) teacher. In addition, the student teacher attends weekly seminars under the direction of the university supervisor. Seminar topics include first day and week of school, teacher ethics, legal rights and responsibilities, classroom management, discipline, classroom organization, public relations, school budgets, evaluating textbooks, ordering supplies, parent conferences, parent orientation, preparing credentials, applying for certification, applying for a job, interviews, and contracts. They also spend a week working with children in an outdoor education experience.

appendix a
Grade Preference Form

The forms and lists in this appendix and those that follow have been used by the authors in their practicums. Each instructor who desires may use them as they are written or adapt them to their individual situations.

Grade Preference Form

Name _____ Section _____

In what grade level (K-6) would you prefer to do your first clinical experience? In the blanks below please indicate these grade levels in order of preference.

Grade _____ Grade _____ Grade _____
       First choice   Second choice   Third choice

Write a paragraph on what you believe are your greatest strengths. Include special talents:

_____

_____

_____

_____

Write a paragraph on what you believe are your weaknesses:

_____

_____

_____

_____

What do you hope to gain from this course?

_____

_____

_____

_____

appendix b
Student Involvement in the Classroom

TO: Cooperating Teachers
FROM: University Supervisor

The following activities are suggested as possible ideas appropriate for the students in this student teaching experience. They are, of course, contingent on how well they work out in your particular classroom.

1. Give individual help to a particular student.

2. Work with a small group of children in an activity you have planned that can readily be picked up and executed by another.

3. Assist in the preparation of teacher-made materials.

4. Acquaint them with your learning center, library and/or media center.

5. Select appropriate books and read orally to the class.**

6. Get children involved in a lesson that can become a bulletin board by the class.

7. Observe the class in another environment (gym, art, music).

8. Share any non-teaching duties you have, such as recess, for them to gain a greater appreciation of the total role of a teacher.

9. Assist and/or administer room duties of attendance taking, lunch count, and distribution of materials, etc.

10. Assist you in getting materials ready for a lesson.

11. Assist with any teacher "housekeeping" jobs.

12. Assist in some correction of student work (but not to the exclusion of other suggestions).

13. Teach a lesson.*

14. Prepare a bulletin board.*

15. Create an educational game.*

16. Do a case study of one child.*

17. Become acquainted with teacher manuals and other classroom materials.

18. Assist with the use of any media equipment.

It would contribute a great deal to the student's learning experience if you would take a few minutes to give him or her constructive feedback after he or she has had an opportunity to actively participate.

---

* Indicates an assignment from the university supervisor.
** Indicates an assignment from an instructor of another related class.

appendix c
Letter of Introduction to Cooperating Teacher

Dear Cooperating Teacher:

Thank you for your willingness to work with one of the first clinical experience students from our university. I hope this experience will prove to be mutually beneficial.

These students are having their first classroom experience. However, since some are transfer students, they may be designated as a junior or a senior by class rank.

I have suggested the following as minimum requirements:

1. A case study of one child. (This is not an in-depth study, but simply an observation of one student throughout the time he or she is there.)
2. Prepare a bulletin board for the classroom.
3. Design a game appropriate for the class level.
4. Prepare at least one lesson of 20-30 minutes that may be taught to the entire class.

All of these requirements are contingent on how well they will work out in your particular classroom. Should you believe any of them are inappropriate or if you have any questions, please let me know.

The students will be in your classroom (dates of student's assigned attendance and names of days) full days.

Enclosed with this letter is an "Information for Cooperating Teacher" form as well as the student assignments. The student will provide you with an evaluation form about a week prior to his or her last day. This form will be due in your school office by 9:00 a.m. on (the student's last day). Should you have any questions, do not hesitate to call me at home, (phone number), or at the office, (phone number). If you cannot reach me and wish me to return your call, you may leave a message at (phone number).

Sincerely,

Name
Professor of Elementary Education

appendix d
Student Information Sheet

Information for Cooperating Teachers:

To the Student: Your cooperating teacher and block instructor need information about you in order to help you. They would appreciate you making informative statements about your present circumstances, your life as a child, your aspirations as a teacher, and other pertinent phases of your life.

Date _____

I. Personal Data

Name _____ Date of Birth _____

Home Address _____ Home Phone _____

City/State/Zip _____

Local Address _____ Local Phone _____

City/State/Zip _____

Can you use a: _____ Typewriter   _____ Film Projector

                  _____ Record Player   _____ Ditto Machine

                  _____ Slide Projector   _____ Tape Recorder

What musical instruments do you play?

_____

_____

What languages do you speak?

_____

_____

What work experiences have you had, summers or after school?

_____

_____

_____

Do you have any physical difficulty or health problems, etc., about which those interested in your personal and professional growth should know?

_____

_____

_____

II. Personal Interests and Activities
    (Tell something about yourself as a person, such as: your favorite forms of relaxation, hobbies, books you enjoy, newspapers and magazines you read, favorite radio and television programs, music you like, traveling you have done, etc.)

III. Experience With Children
    (Describe contacts or experiences you have had outside of school. These may include experiences with brothers and sisters, as a camp counselor, with young cousins or other relatives, as a scout leader, baby-sitting, etc. Please be fairly definite as to the age of the children, the kind of responsibility, and the extent of your contacts.)

IV. Family and Community Background (optional)
    (Pertinent information may include such items as national backgrounds, education and occupation of your parents, number and ages of brothers and sisters, others who are living or have lived at your home, languages spoken in your home, types of communities in which you have lived, and community activities in which members of your family participate.)

V. School Life Prior to College
    (Include relevant information about kindergarten and nursery school attendance, size and location of elementary schools attended, outstanding experiences during elementary school, childhood organizations such as scouts, 4-H, etc., to which you belonged, high school attended, curriculum and major subjects in high school, teachers you remember, high school activities and organizations in which you were active, etc.).

VII. College Life
      (Helpful information may include membership in college organizations, nature of participation in each organization, writing for college publications, participation in musical and dramatic performances, experiences in dormitory living or rooming in town, employment while in school, etc.)

VIII. General Statement About Yourself as a Future Teacher
       (Discuss why you want to be a teacher, people who have influenced you to teach, contacts with teachers outside of school, etc.)

appendix e
Bulletin Board Resources

The following books are available from Carson-Dellosa Publishing Company, Greensboro, North Carolina 27416:

Carson, P., & Dellosa, J. (1979). *Holiday Bulletin Board and Art Activities*, 63 pages. Includes bulletin board characters and related projects for each season.

————(1989). *Tree Bulletin Board and Art Projects*, 160 pages. Contains two tree patterns with twelve tree bulletin boards and twelve additional ideas and patterns. Each project includes a border, an art project, two worksheets, and a related reward.

————(1989). *Bulletin Board Magic*, (K-12), 384 pages. Format similar to above listing.

————(1984). *Preschool, Kindergarten Bulletin Boards and More,* 64 pages. Contains 21 different themes. Example: "I Know My Left (Hand) From My Right."

The following books are available from Education Center Inc., Greensboro, North Carolina 27420:

Education Center Inc. (1991). *Bulletin Boards Your Little Kids Can Make*, 192 pages. Designed for preschool, kindergarten and first grade. Includes sixty-two bulletin boards with patterns, awards, extension activities, and variations. Six ideas for each month.

————(1987). *Bulletin Boards Your Kids Can Make*, 1987 pages. Designed for K-4. Format similar to above.

The following books are available from Evan-Moor Corporation, 9425 York Road, Monterey, California 93940:

Evans, J., & Moore, J.E. (1983). *A Bulletin Board for the WHOLE Year*, (K-3), 35 pages. Calendar board ideas for September-June.

————(1983). *Bulletin Boards That Teach,* 60 pages.

Moore, J.E., & Morgan, K. (1988). *Seasonal Bulletin Boards*, 88 pages. Designed for K-6. Contains ideas for boards for every month and gives ideas for changing the board during the month.

The following books are available from Fearon Teacher-Aid, 500 Harbor Blvd., Belmont, California 94002:

Flores, A. (1979). *Instant Borders*, 81 pages. Contains border ideas.

————(1983). *Instant Bulletin Boards*, 139 pages. Quick and easy methods for preparing borders, letters, figures, calendars, and calendar keepers.

The following books are available from Incentive Publications, Box 12522, Nashville, Tennessee 37212:

Brisson, L. (1988). 3-D Bulletin Boards, 78 pages. All bulletin boards are 3-D or have manipulative parts. Includes six subject matter, five skill, and seven seasonal bulletin boards.

Forte, I. (1987). *Early Learning Bulletin Boards*, 63 pages.

————(1987). *Fall Bulletin Boards*, 63 pages.

————(1986). *Holiday and Seasonal Bulletin Boards*, 64 pages.

————(1986). *Math Bulletin Boards*, 64 pages.

————(1986). *Reading Bulletin Boards,* 64 pages.

————(1986). *Science Bulletin Boards*, 64 pages.

————(1987). *Spring bulletin boards,* 63 pages.

————(1987). *Winter Bulletin Boards*, 63 pages.

All of the Forte books contain excellent patterns.

Michener, D., & Maschlitz, B. (1981). *Bulletin Board Bonanza,* 96 pages.

Richards, J., & Stanley, M. (1986). *School Spirit and Self-Esteem Bulletin Boards.* Includes a list of materials, and directions needed for assembly.

The following books are available from Frank Schaeffer Publications, 1028 Via Mirabel, Palos Verde Estates, Georgia 90274:

Gruber, B., & Gruber, S. (1989). *Holiday and Seasonal Bulletin Boards,* 64 pages. Includes nine ideas for fall, ten for winter, and eight for spring.

————(1987). *Easy Bulletin Boards,* 64 pages. Includes four ideas each for fall, winter, and spring. Thirteen ideas for use any time.

The following books are available from Good Apple Inc., Box 299, Carthage, Illinois 62321:

> Filkins, V., & Spizman, R. (1989). *Bulletin Boards Plus*, 106 pages.
>
> Finton, E. (1979). *Bulletin Boards Should Be More Than Something To Look At,* 56 pages.
>
> Spizman, R. (1984). *Bulletin Boards,* 60 pages. Seasonal ideas and activities.
>
> ———(1981). *Bulletin Board Bonanzas,* 138 pages. For intermediate grades.
>
> Spizman, R., & Pesiri, E. (1983). *All Aboard with Bulletin Boards*, 90 pages.

The following books are available from The Learning Works, P.O. Box 6178, Santa Barbara, California 93160:

> Armstrong, B., & Butterfield, S. (1985). *Borders and Beyond,* 48 pages. An excellent collection of border patterns in a variety of creative shapes. Example: A bulletin board entitled "Brush Up on Fractions" is bordered with large brushes.
>
> Glover, S., & Grewe, G. (1982). *Holiday Happenings,* 111 pages. Includes seasonal bulletin boards as well as related art projects and activities.
>
> ———(1982). *Bulletin Board Smorgasbord,* 112 pages. Seventy separate ideas to reinforce basic concepts in language arts, math, science, and social studies. Includes detailed drawings, assembly instructions and suggestions for use.

The following book is available from Scholastic Inc., E. McCarty Street, Jefferson City, Missouri 65102:

> Instructor, (1987). *Blockbuster Bulletin Boards,* 192 pages. Includes three hundred and fifty seasonal and subject matter ideas.

The following books are available from Trellis Books, Canandaigua, New York 14424:

> Molyneux, L., & Marasea, P. (1986). *Lifesavers: A Year of Bulletin Boards, Games and Activities*, 188 pages.
>
> Molylneux, L. (1983). *Getting It Together,* 160 pages. Many ideas for group projects for creative bulletin boards.

appendix f
Game Resources

Fearon Teacher Aids Pitman Learning Inc., Belmont, California

>Love, M. (1983). *Twenty Word Structure Games*, grades 2-6, 120 pages.

Good Apple Inc., Box 299, Carthage, Illinois 62321

>Heit, B. (Sister) (1980). *Gameboards For Everyone*, Grades K-6, 180 pages.

Illinois State Board of Education, Department of Specialized Educational Services, 100 North First Street, Springfield, Illinois 62704

>(1982). *Share and Tell*, teacher-made materials, 125 pages.

Incentive Publications Inc., Box 12522, Nashville, Tennessee 37212

>Lill, S., & Vittitow, M.L. (1985). *Learning Games Without Losers*, 95 pages.

The Learning Works, P.O. Box 6178, Santa Barbara, California 93160

>Isaak, B., & Armstrong, B. (1982). *Garbage Games*, 112 pages. Makes games from usable, though usually discarded, materials.

appendix g
Learning Center Resources

Allyn and Bacon Inc., 7 Wells Avenue, Newton, Massachusetts 02159

Tiedt, S.W., Tiedt, I.M. (1978). *Language Arts Activities*, 359 pages.

Good Apple, Inc. Box 299, Carthage, Illinois 62321

Glover, S., & Grewe, G. (1987). A splash of spring, grades 2-5, 120 pages. Learning center activities in a variety of content areas focused on spring.

Goodyear Publishing Company Inc., Santa Monica, California 90401

Breyfogle, E., Nelson, S., Pitts, C., & Santich, P. (1976). *Creating a Learning Environment*, 280 pages. Ideas for language arts, reading, and math at each of three levels: kindergarten, primary and intermediate.

Incentive Publications, Box 12522, Nashville, Tennessee 37212

Catalog of all *Kid's Stuff* material—no charge, write to above address.

Kid's Stuff: Reading and Writing Readiness

Kid's Stuff: Kindergarten and Nursery School

Kid's Stuff: Intermediate-Junior High

Kid's Stuff: Math

Creative Science Experiences

Creative Math Experiences

Nooks, Crannies, and Corners

Center Stuff for Nooks, Crannies, and Corners

More Center Stuff for Nooks, Crannies, and Corners

Cornering Creative Writing

Pumpkins, Pinwheels, and Peppermint Packages

Forte, I. *Patters, Projects and Plans*, approximately 180 pages. Published monthly. Name of month precedes title. Good ideas for learning centers, also bulletin boards.

Frank, M., Illustrator, Howard, J. (1979). *If You're Trying to Teach Kids How to Write, You've Gotta Have This Book*, 215 pages. Great ideas for creative writing—both for teaching it, and for use in learning centers.

Michener, D., & Muschllitz, B. (1979). *Teacher's Gold Mine*, 223 pages.

Teachers Friend Publications, 11521 Davis Street, Moreno, California 92387

Sevaly, K. *Idea Book*. This is a creative idea book published monthly for the elementary teacher. Preceding the title will be the name of the month, example: "October Idea Book." They contain 100-115 pages. This has a variety of uses.

appendix h
Sorting Out Objectives

I want to be more...

I want to be in a position that will allow me to...

I want to feel...

I want to quit...

I want to lose...

I want to be able to...

I want to get out from under the pressure of...

I want to be more in control of...

I want to develop my...

I want to get on top of...

I want to improve my...

I want to finish...

I want to become...

I want to change...

I want to begin...

Marvin Fogel, Ph.D.
Human Service Consultants
Sycamore, Illinois 60178

bibliography

The following bibliography includes references for additional reading. The authors have included books and articles they believe will be beneficial in your student teaching experience and as you enter the teaching profession.

Periodicals

Atwell, Nancy. "Teaching and Whole Language." *Instructor* (November/December 1992): 48, 49.

Bluestein, Jane. "Great Expectations." *Instructor* 95 (August 1985): 36-40.

Bracey, G. W. "Books and Literature as Partners in Research." *Phi Delta Kappan* 73 (December 1992): 344-346.

————. "What's Right With Madeline Hunter?" *Phi Delta Kappan* 69 (January 1988): 378,379.

————. "Whole Language versus Code Orientation." *Phi Delta Kappan* 74 (September 1992): 87,88.

Brown, Jim, and William Kritsonis. "Teachers: Don't Be Part of the Discipline Problem." *The Education Digest* 58 (December 1992): 51-55.

Burns, Brendon. "In New Zealand, Good Reading and Writing Come Naturally." *Newsweek* 118 (Dec. 2, 1991): 53.

Dill, Isaac. "Describe Your Favorite Teacher." *Educational Leadership* 50 (March 1993): 54.

Dunn, Rita, and Kenneth Dunn. "Ten Ways to Make the Classroom a Better Place to Learn." *Instructor* 94 (November/December 1984): 84-88, 139.

Epstein, Joyce. "Making Parents Your Partners." *Instructor* (April 1993): 52,53.

Flexer, Roberta, and Naomi Rosenberger. "Beware of Tapping Pencils." *Arithmetic Teacher* 34 (January 1987): 6-10.

Gawranski, Jane D. "One Point of View: Great Theory; Why Little Impact?" *Arithmetic Teacher* 34 (January 1987): 2-4.

Goodblad. "A Study of the Education of Educators One Year *Later*." *Phi Delta Kappan* 73 (December 1991): 311-316.

Gorman, N. B., and H. M. Hazi. "Teachers Ask: Is There Life After Madeline Hunter?" *Phi Delta Kappan* 69 (May 1988): 669-672.

Groen, G. J., and J. M. Parkman. "A Chrometric Analysis of Simple Addition." *Psychological Review* 79 (July 1972): 329-343.

Houlihan, D. M., and H. P. Ginsburg. "The Addition Methods of First and Second Grade Children." *Journal for Research in Mathematics Education* 12 (March 1981): 95-106.

Hunter, Madeline, and Doug Russell. "Planning for Effective Instruction." *Instructor* (September 1977).

Kramer, Terence, and David A. Krug. "A Rationale and Procedure for Teaching Addition." *Education and Training of the Mentally Retarded* 8 (October 1973): 140-145.

Langlois, Donald, and Charlotte Zales. "Anatomy of a Top Teacher." *The American School Board Journal* 178 (August 1991): 44-46.

Moyers, Susanne. "Bridging the Culture Gap." *Instructor* (January 1993): 31-33.

O'Keefe, Tim. "A Year in the Life of a Whole Language Teacher." *Instructor* (November/December 1992): 44-47.

Sanacore, Joseph. "Whole Language Grouping That Works." *Reading and Writing Quarterly* 8 (July/September 1992): 295-303.

Shively, Judith. "Why I Entered Teaching, Why I Stay." *Educational Leadership* 49 (November 1991): 84-86.

Slavin, R. E. "Pet and the Pendulum: Faddism in Education and How to Stop it." *Phi Delta Kappan* 70 (January 1989): 752-758.

Stansbury, Michelle. "Cooperative Learning." *Instructor* (September 1992): 53,54.

Suydam, Marilyn. "Research Report: Improving Multiplication Skills." *Arithmetic Teacher* 32 (March 1985): 52.

Vandergrift, Judith A., and Andrea Greene. "Rethinking Parent Involvement." *Educational Leadership* 50 (September 1992): 57-59.

Walter, Glenn. "A Veteran's Advice to Rookies." *Instructor* 92 (August 1982): 48.

Webster, William. "Thank You, Miss Monroe." *Educational Leadership* 50 (April 1993): 45.

Wherry, John S. "Getting Parents Involved." *Vocational Educational Journal* 66 (September 1991): 34-55.

Books

Adams, Dennis M., and Mary E. Hamm. *Cooperative Learning and Collaboration Across the Curriculum.* Springfield, Ill.: Charles C. Thomas, 1990.

> A practical guide to instructional methods in basic skill areas. The book provides examples using cooperative models and strategies for teaching critical thinking skills.

Ballare, Antonia, and Angelique Lampros. *The Classroom Organizer.* West Nyack, NY: Parker Publishing Company, 1989.

> This publication contains two-hundred and one ready-to-use forms for K-8 teachers and administrators. It has more value for the beginning teacher than to the student teacher, but certain forms could be adapted.

Baratta-Lorton, Mary. *Mathematics Their Way: An Activity Centered Mathematic Program.* Addison Wesley, 1976.

Barzun, Jacques. *Begin Here: The Forgotten Conditions of Teaching and Learning.* Chicago: The University of Chicago Press, 1991.

> "The sole justification of teaching, of the school itself," Barzun writes, "is that the student comes out of it able to do something he could not do before." This book offers guidelines for resolving the problems in today's schools.

Bell, Irene, and Jeanne E. Wieckert. *Basic Media Skills Through Games.* Littleton, Colo.: Libraries Unlimited Inc., 1985.

> One hundred forty-two games that can be used to teach a variety of skills in the media center, or the classroom.

Board, John C. (ed.) *A Special Relationship: Our Teachers and How We Learned.* New York: Pushcart Press, 1991.

> An anthology of teachers and their students, and the special relationship between them.

Bullock, Jan, et. al. *Touch Math Teacher's Manual.* Colorado Springs, Colo.: Touch Math, 1981.

Canter, Lee, and Marlene Canter. *Assertive Discipline.* Santa Monica, Calif.: Canter and Associates, 1986.

> An excellent book for the student or beginning teacher. The book advocates a systematic approach to discipline, and provides the ideas and the skills needed.

Chernow, Fred, and Carol Chernow. *Classroom Discipline and Control.* West Nyack, NY: Parker Publishing Company, 1981.

A practical handbook containing a collection of classroom-tested methods that will enable the teacher to take control.

Cozic, Charles (ed.). *Education in America.* San Diego, Calif.: Greenhaven Press, 1992.

This book is part of the "opposing viewpoints" series, developed to help the reader become more informed on issues in education today. The chapters on "How Can The Teaching Profession Be Improved?" and "Should Education for Minority Students Emphasize Ethnicity?" will be especially interesting for the student teacher.

Cullim, Albert. *The Geranium on the Window Sill Just Died But Teacher You Went Right On.* Holland: Harline Quest Inc., 1971.

An excellent book, recalls how it felt to be a child—small, awkward and powerless—and reminds us that children still feel that way.

Davidson, Neil, and Toni Worsham (ed.) *Enhancing Thinking Through Cooperative Learning.* New York: Teachers College Press, 1992.

An excellent resource for the student interested in learning more about cooperative learning, and how to help students think more effectively.

Donavin, Denise. *Best of the Best for Children.* New York: Random House, 1992.

A resource of children's literature.

Farber, Barry A. *Stress and Burnout in the American Teacher.* San Francisco: Jassey-Boss Publishers, 1991.

Farber looks at the problem of teacher stress and shows how the events of the past thirty years have intensified the problems. The book offers alternatives to combat burnout.

Ginot, Haim G. *Teacher and Child.* New York: Macmillan Publishing Co., 1972.

Student teachers will find this a book with practical solutions for dealing with the daily situations faced by all teachers. Every teacher should read Ginot's quotation in the preface which sums up the books, and Ginot's philosophy.

Godor, John. *Teachers Talk.* Macomb, Ill.: Glenbridge Publishing Ltd., 1990.

Interviews with two-hundred and eighty two teachers from 30 different school districts, using their words to discuss the idealism that brought them into teaching, and some of the disillusion they now experience. A good resource for the student considering teaching as a career.

Hearndon, James. *Notes from a School Teacher.* New York: Simon and Schuster, 1985.

> A teacher with twenty-five years of experience writes about the children and the system.

Johnson, David, et. al. *Cooperating in the Classroom.* Edina, Minn.: Interaction Book Company, 1988.

> The book contains a set of practical strategies for structuring cooperative learning groups.

Johnson, Lou Anne. *My Posse Don't Do Homework.* New York: St. Martins, 1992.

> An inspiring account of how one teacher met the challenges of the classroom.

Kabrin, David. *In There With the Kids.* New York: Houghton Mifflin Co., 1992.

> Kabrin uses the format of two caring fictional teachers to raise questions about how teaching leads to learning. As Kabrin says, "One of the beautiful things about teaching is that everyone gets to try again."

Kohl, Herbert. *Growing Minds: On Becoming a Teacher.* New York: Harper and Row.

> A must read for the student teacher on the challenge of teaching. Part 4, "Why Teach?" should be required reading for all teachers.

Komiya, Art. *Elementary Teacher's Handbook of Indoor and Outdoor Games.* West Nyack, NY: Parker Publishing Company, 1985.

> Good variety of games for inside and outside the classroom.

Kounin, Jacob. *Discipline and Group Management in Classrooms.* New York: Holt Rhineheart and Winston, 1970.

> Kounin's research into group management in the classroom attempts to answer the questions of classroom discipline.

Kramer, Rita. *Ed School Follies: The Miseducation of America's Teachers.* New York: The Free Press, a division of Macmillan, 1991.

> A study of fifteen schools of education throughout the United States, this book provides a look at the follies of our educational establishment.

Long, James D., and Virginia H. Frye. *Making it Till Friday: A Guide to Successful Classroom Management.* New Jersey: Princeton Book Co., 1989.

> An excellent book for the beginning teacher who wants to know more about classroom management.

Malehorn, Hal. *Elementary Teacher's Classroom Management Handbook.* West Nyack, NY: Parker Publishing Co., 1984.

This book provides the teacher with nearly one thousand suggestions to simplify the tasks of the classroom. Ideas cover classroom environment, curriculum, and organization.

Mahn, Karen. *Behavior Management in K-6 Classrooms.* Washington, D.C.: National Educational Association of the United States, 1992.

The system of classroom management advocated in this publication is the concept of planning ahead to prevent behavior problems. Contains some ideas useful to all teachers.

McElmeel, Sharron. *My Bag of Book Tricks.* Englewood, Colo.: Teacher Idea Press, 1989.

A wealth of ideas for using literature in the classroom, as well as extensive book lists. A great resource for the teacher of whole language.

Norton, Donna. *The Impact of Literature-Based Reading.* New York: Macmillan Publishing Co., 1992.

Another excellent resource for the literature-based program. This book focuses on a variety of activities and literature emphasizing teacher direction, student interaction, and independent reading.

Ortman, Patricia, *Not for Teachers Only: Creating a Context of Joy for Learning and Growth.* Washington D.C.: 1988.

A requirement for every teacher's library, the author is not only inspiring, but gives the beginning teacher some excellent ideas for creating the proper emotional climate in the classroom.

Sabil, Max, and Evan M. Motelisky. *Teaching Mathematics.* New Jersey: Prentice Hall, 1975.

A sourcebook of aids, activities, and strategies for teaching mathematics. Appropriate for intermediate or junior high school students.

Wolfgang, Charles, and Carl D. Glickman. *Solving Discipline Problems: Strategies for Classroom Teachers.* Boston: Allyn and Bacon, 1986.

An excellent resource for the student who wants to study the operational models of discipline as well as the various approaches.

Index

Notes

Notes

Notes

Notes

Notes

Notes

Notes

Notes

Notes

Notes

Notes

Notes

Notes

Notes

Notes

Notes

Notes

Notes

Notes

Notes

Notes

Notes